BABY meal PLANNER

Nicola Graimes

This is a Parragon Book

This edition published in 2002

Parragon
Queen Street House
4 Queen Street
Bath, BA1 1HE UK

Designed by The Bridgewater Book Company

Art Director Terry Jeavons
Editorial Director Fiona Biggs
Senior Designer Colin Fielder
Editor Sarah Bragginton
Page Layout Jane and Chris Lanaway
Picture Research Liz Moore
Photography David Jordan
Home Economist Sarah Lewis
Illustrations Rhian Nest-James

Printed and bound in Spain

ISBN 0-75257-929-0

This book uses metric and imperial measurements. Follow the same units of measurement throughout; do not mix metric and imperial. All spoon measurements are level: teaspoons are assumed to be 5 ml and tablespoons are assumed to be 15 ml. Unless otherwise stated, milk is assumed to be full fat, eggs and individual vegetables such as potatoes are medium, and pepper is freshly ground black pepper.

The times given for each recipe are an approximate guide only because the preparation times may differ according to the techniques used by different people and the cooking times may vary as a result of the type of oven used.

contents

Introduction

Having a baby is a bit like being on a rollercoaster; no sooner have you mastered (or at least become accustomed to) breast or bottle feeding, than it's time to tackle a new stage in your baby's development – weaning. I can remember feeling distinctly nervy about the prospect of introducing solids to my daughter's diet.

Queries such as when to introduce solids, which first foods are best and how much my baby should eat immediately sprang to mind, and just to confuse matters further, there seemed to be a plethora of well-meaning advice. For example, in the recent past there was a lot of pressure on parents to start their babies on solid food much earlier than 4 months – this pressure came from various camps: commercial, medical and social. Ideas have now changed, however, and this is all to the good. Many quite ordinary foods can cause allergies, and a baby's digestive system is incapable, at least until 3 months old, of absorbing foods more complex than baby milk. But fear not, however momentous this stage may seem, it is vital to bear in mind that weaning is a gradual

BELOW *Try not to worry too much about weaning: if you are relaxed, then your baby will be too.*

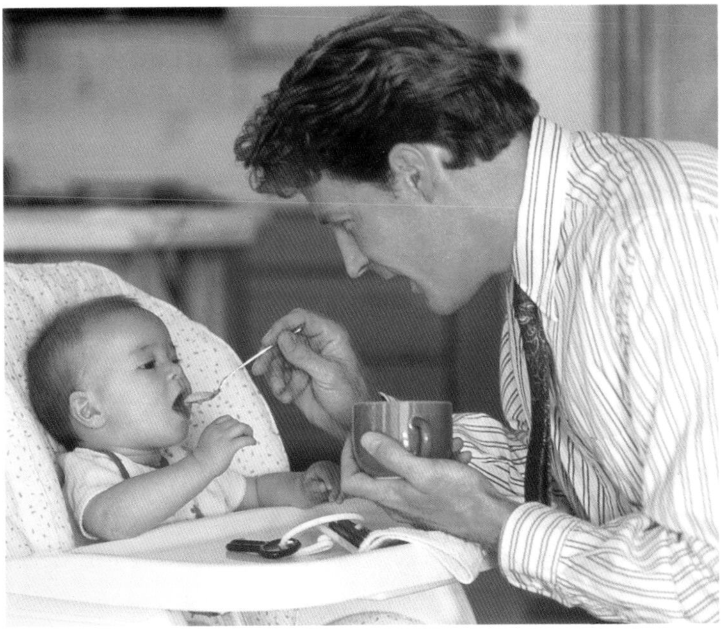

ABOVE *Introduce a new food a spoon at a time – this way, it is much more manageable for your child.*

process and, if embarked on with a certain amount of knowledge and optimism, it can be a fulfiling and fun experience for baby and parents alike.

The aim of this book is to ease any anxieties you may have, as well as smooth the path from your baby's first taste of solids to his or her participating in family meals. The advice is designed to be practical and reassuring, to help you give your baby the best start in life. Many parents feel that they don't have the required time or cookery skills to make home-made baby foods, but first foods couldn't be easier to make and, especially if prepared in bulk, take the minimum amount of time. By making your own foods you can also familiarise your baby with a wide range of tastes and textures.

Every baby and toddler is different, with his or her own particular likes and dislikes, which can sometimes change on a daily basis. It wasn't unusual for my daughter to absolutely adore a particular food to the extent she couldn't eat enough of it, then to turn up her nose the next time she was offered it. Most parents will vouch that this behaviour is common. However perturbed or frustrated you may feel, it is counter-productive to force your baby to eat and can lead to mealtimes becoming a type of power game. Many parents recall times when their child ate nothing but toast for weeks without any adverse effects, which is reassuring.

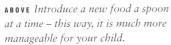

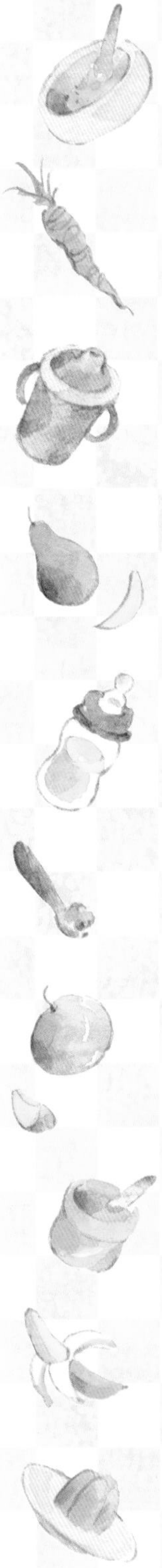

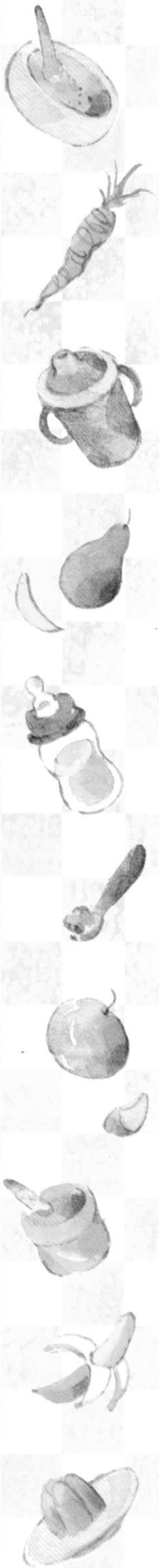

What do Babies Need?

While the saying 'you are what you eat' may be an overused cliché, it's not far from the truth. Health experts now suggest that what we eat in childhood has implications for our future health. Consequently, it's crucial for parents to encourage their child to enjoy a varied diet as soon as possible.

MILK

For the first six months of your baby's life, breast or formula milk provides all the nutrients and nourishment he or she needs for growth and development. Breast or formula milk should form a major part of his or her life up until a year old, when cow's milk can be introduced as a drink.

Experts firmly believe that breast milk is best for a baby, since it provides the correct balance of vitamins, minerals and fats in a readily digestible form. Breast milk contains the antibodies necessary to help fight off infections, and research shows that it may also improve mental development in the long term.

At some stage you may wish to introduce a bottle for at least some of the milk feeds if, for instance, you are returning to work. This transition will take time, so be patient with yourself and your baby.

BREADS AND CEREALS

Otherwise known as starchy foods, breads and cereals are among the best sources of energy, vitamins, minerals and fibre. Bread, pasta, rice, potatoes and low sugar breakfast cereals should form a major part of any meal. Do not give wheat-based foods to babies under six months.

FRUIT AND VEGETABLES

Fresh and frozen, and to a lesser extent canned, fruit and vegetables are an essential part of a baby's diet. They are the perfect first foods, providing rich amounts of vitamins, minerals and fibre. From six months, try to give at least four to five different types of fresh produce a day to your baby.

MEAT, FISH, EGGS AND VEGETARIAN ALTERNATIVES

These are a good source of protein, essential for growth and repair. Your child should be given a protein food at every meal but it is vital to offer a good variety, including beans, lentils and soya-based foods.

DAIRY FOODS

Milk, cheese and yogurt provide protein, vitamins and minerals, particularly calcium for healthy bones and teeth. Cow's milk can be used in cooking from six months, but is not to be given as a drink before a year old, when full-cream milk can be introduced. Skimmed cow's milk is not recommended before your child is five years old, since it lacks the energy a growing child requires.

SWEET FOODS

Babies seem to have a naturally sweet tooth and the sweetness of breast milk may be partly to blame. There's nothing wrong with the occasional sweet treat but sugar can rot the teeth.

SALTY FOODS

Don't add salt to food for babies and young children as their kidneys are insufficiently mature to cope. If you are cooking for the whole family, separate your child's portion before adding any seasoning. Salt is added to many commercial foods, and stocks and yeast-based spreads can contain excessive amounts, so look for low salt alternatives or use them sparingly.

IRON

Babies are born with a store of iron and the mineral is also found in breast and formula milk. However, by about six months, most babies have used up their iron reserves and even if they are drinking iron-fortified milk, it is important to include foods rich in the mineral in their diet.

Good sources include:

- red meat
- liver
- fish
- eggs
- beans and lentils
- leafy green vegetables
- wholegrain cereals
- fortified breakfast cereals
- dried fruit, especially apricots

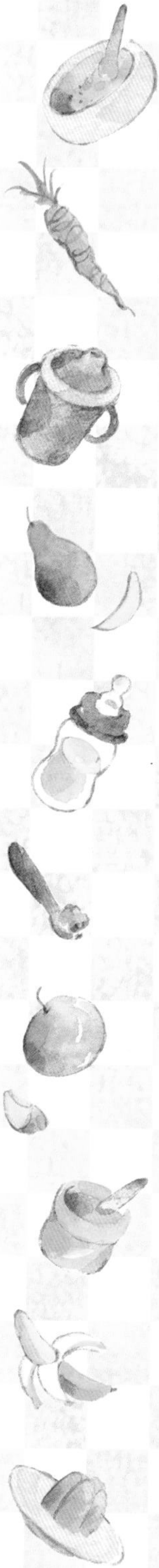

Cooking for your Baby

Ideally, every morsel that passed your baby's lips would be home-prepared, but this is unrealistic for most of us. Having said this, it's vital to provide as much fresh, unprocessed food as possible, and the recipes in this book have been created to help even the busiest parent. They don't require hours of preparation or slaving over a hot stove and most are suitable for home freezing.

FRESH IS BEST

Many of us fall into the trap of believing our little ones prefer so-called 'children's food', and pander to our expectations by buying foods that we would not normally even contemplate. Experts firmly believe that good eating habits are formed early, so it's important for we parents to provide a variety of foods, encompassing a whole different range of flavours, colours and textures. I was certainly surprised to find that my daughter loved strongly flavoured and quite highly spiced foods, especially curries and anything that contained onion and garlic.

COMMERCIAL FOODS

Lack of time and energy leads many of us to resort to the easy option. However, now is not the time to feel guilty – the occasional packet or jar will not

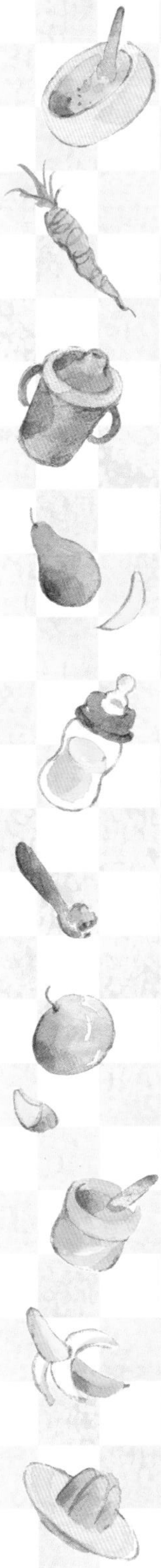

LEFT *Discuss any dietary or nutritional worries you have about your baby with your health visitor.*

BELOW *Becoming more aware of what's in the food you eat can help you shop more healthily.*

harm a baby's health, but relying on them 100 per cent might. When buying commercial baby foods, it is advisable to check the label for unwanted additives, sugars (sucrose, dextrose, glucose), artificial sweeteners, salt and thickeners such as modified starch, which simply bulk out ingredients. Instead opt for brands – especially the organic ones – that are free from additives and are without added salt, sugar and sweeteners.

ALLERGIES

It is suggested that the number of children with food intolerances is on the increase, yet it is true that life-threatening allergies are extremely rare. In children the most commonly responsible foods are cow's milk, gluten, eggs, seafood, peanuts, tomatoes, sugar and strawberries, with symptoms ranging from rashes, upset stomachs and hyperactivity to asthma, eczema, breathing difficulties and swelling of the throat. If you have a history of food allergies in the family or suspect a problem with a particular food and are very concerned, it is advisable to talk to your health visitor or doctor.

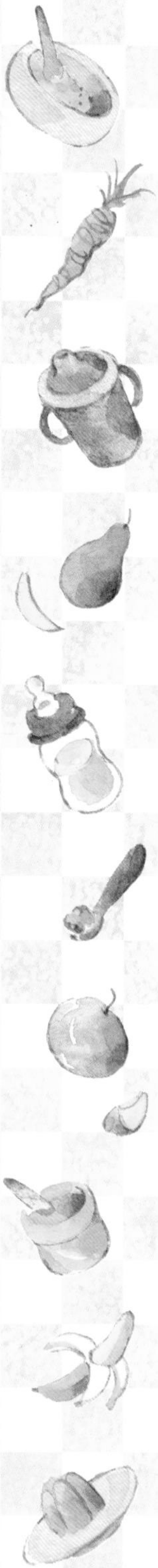

First Foods

A common question from new mothers is 'when can I introduce certain foods?' The following list is a good starting point but is not exhaustive. Use this chart as a guide, adapting it according to what is in season and what you are preparing for your family at the time.

STAGES OF WEANING

FOODS	DRINKS
4-5 MONTHS	
Thin, smooth purées.	Breast or formula milk – about five feeds a day.
5-6 MONTHS	
Thicker, smooth purées.	Breast or formula milk – about five feeds a day.
6-9 MONTHS	
Six to eight months: coarsely puréed food. **Eight to nine months:** mashed or minced foods.	Breast, formula or follow-on milk – about four feeds a day, cooled boiled water, diluted unsweetened fruit juice (1 part juice: 5 parts water).
9-12 MONTHS	
Chopped foods.	Breast, formula or follow-on milk – about three feeds a day, cooled boiled water, diluted unsweetened fruit juice (1 part juice: 5 parts water).
12-18 MONTHS	
Chopped foods.	Breast, formula or follow-on milk – about two feeds a day, cooled boiled water, diluted unsweetened fruit juice (1 part juice: 5 parts water).

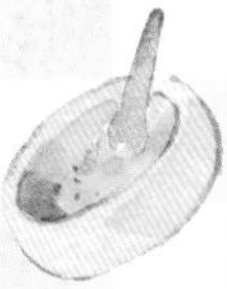

DRINKS

Generally babies under 6 months do not need additional drinks but if your baby is thirsty between feeds, offer cooled, boiled water rather than sugary drinks. There are many commercial baby drinks available but most of them, including herbal ones, are laden with sugar. Artificial sweeteners are no better since they can upset the stomach. If you do offer your baby fruit juice, it is advisable to dilute it with water (1 part juice to 5 parts water). Offer drinks in a feeder cup or beaker rather than a bottle from six months to avoid the risk of dental decay.

Suitable drinks breast, formula or follow-on milk, water, very dilute, unsweetened fruit juice.

Unsuitable drinks sweetened fruit juice, squash, drinks with artificial sweeteners, tea, coffee, cola and other fizzy drinks, alcohol.

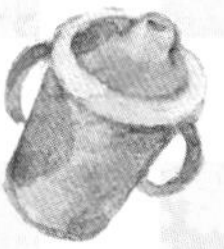

SHOPPING LIST	FOODS TO AVOID
Short-grain white rice, apples, bananas, pears, potatoes, carrots, sweet potatoes, courgettes. Thin porridge can be made from cornmeal, sago and millet.	Salt, sugar, dairy foods, eggs, meat, fish and shellfish, citrus fruit, wheat-based foods and those containing gluten, nuts, fatty foods, spices, chilli, broccoli, sprouts, cabbage and spinach.
Same foods as for four to five months plus avocado, mango, melon, dried apricots, prunes, pears, peaches, broccoli, peas, cauliflower, leeks, apricots, swede, spinach, French beans, parsnips and squash.	Salt, sugar, dairy foods, meat, fish and shellfish, eggs, citrus fruit, wheat-based foods and those containing gluten, nuts, fatty foods and spices, especially chilli.
Fruits, vegetables, dairy products such as fromage frais, yogurt and milk puddings, cow's milk (use in cooking), wheat, eggs (well-cooked yolk), smooth peanut butter, lentils, beans and chicken. Cheese, meat and fish from eight months.	Cow's milk (as a drink), whole nuts, shellfish, egg white, soft or blue cheese, chillies, salt and sugar.
Fruits, vegetables, meat, chicken, fish, dairy products such as cheese, yogurt and milk puddings, wheat, eggs, smooth peanut butter, fish, lentils and beans.	Raw eggs, shellfish, whole nuts, chillies, salt, cow's milk as a drink, soft and blue cheese.
Same as family.	Whole nuts, chillies and raw eggs.

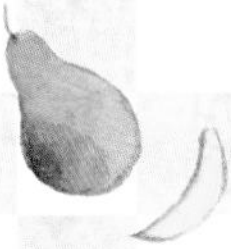

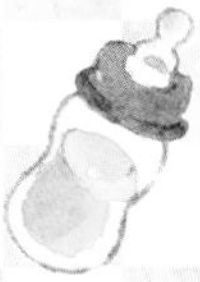

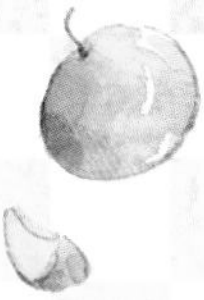

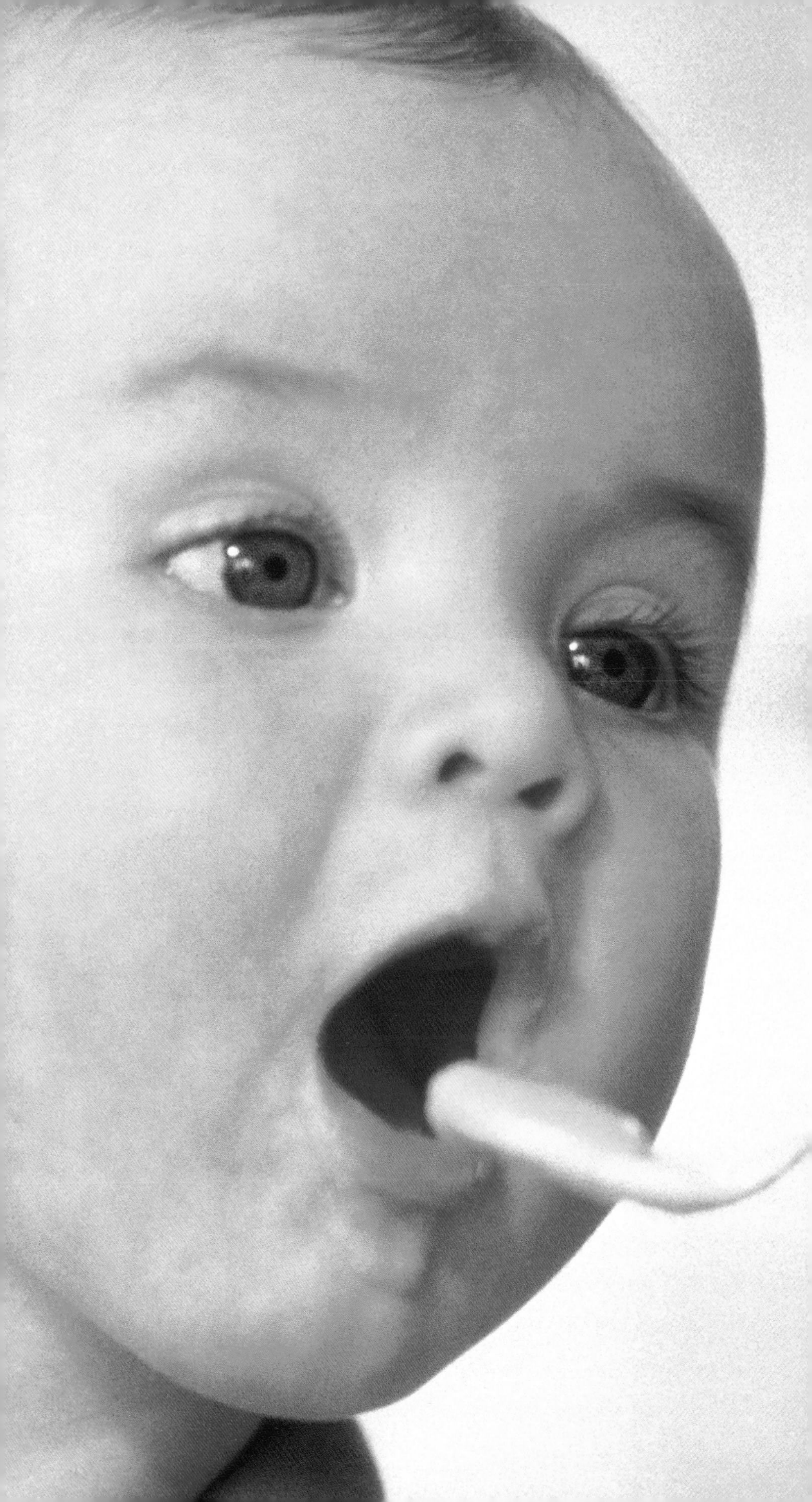

SECTION ONE

four to six months

Weaning is the gradual process of reducing a baby's total dependence on milk to eating a full and varied diet, eventually with the rest of the family. However daunting this may first sound, the process of introducing so-called 'solids' – actually purées – is in fact very simple. The most important piece of advice is relax and don't panic. Remember, food should be one of life's pleasures.

Is Your Baby Ready?

Your baby is ready to take his or her first spoonful from age four to six months. Experts agree that a baby's digestive system is too immature for solids before four months, and early weaning can put stress on the kidneys, as well as triggering possible allergies. Breast or formula milk provides all the nutrients a baby needs for the first six months.

All babies are different and progress at their own pace, but the following may indicate that your baby is ready for solids:

- starts waking in the night, after initially sleeping through
- seems unsatisfied after a milk feed and hungrier than usual
- starts to demand more frequent feeds than usual
- shows an interest in your food

WEANING GUIDELINES

It is worth reiterating that milk provides everything your baby requires for the first six months. Bear this in mind and weaning becomes less intimidating, since it really doesn't matter if your baby doesn't take to solids initially. The following may help:

- Don't force feed your baby: eating is a new skill, which must be accomplished gradually. Your baby is exercising previously unused muscles and will initially try to suck food, which explains why it is often pushed right out of the mouth or appears to be 'spat' out.
- Be scrupulous with hygiene: make sure all spoons and bowls are sterilised and don't store any leftover food for later use as it could be a breeding ground for bacteria. Give your baby his or her own eating utensils.
- Choose the right time to introduce solids: it's important to pick a time when you're not rushed and your baby is not feeling too tired or hungry – the middle of the day is often seen as the best option for both of you. It may be a good idea to give your baby a little milk first to curb any hunger pangs, but as feeding becomes established, start to offer food before milk.
- Face-to-face interaction is important: try to be as encouraging as possible when you are offering new tastes to your baby by smiling and making loving sounds. Let him or her see you eating too.

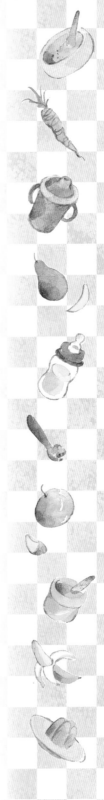

ABOVE *If you are relaxed when you are feeding your baby, he or she will be comfortable with the idea too.*

FIRST FOODS

To begin, offer a little baby rice or a fruit or vegetable purée (see recipe section) on the tip of a shallow plastic spoon or your finger. Commercial baby rice is readily available but it is also simple and quick to prepare your own, and then freeze it in convenient-sized portions. Don't expect your baby to eat more than a tablespoon or even less – at this stage, the amount that is eaten is immaterial.

For the first three weeks, offer the same food for around three days at a time to enable your baby to get used to new tastes and for you to gauge if there is any form of allergic reaction. Thin and runny single-ingredient purées made from fairly mild-tasting fruits and vegetables such as potatoes, carrots, apples and bananas are best. Wash the fruit or vegetables thoroughly and peel them, removing any core or pips. By the fourth or fifth week, and if your baby is happily accepting the food that you are offering him or her, you can start to increase the number of solid feeds from one to three a day. Water or diluted fruit juice can now replace the lunchtime milk feed. Again, introduce new foods gradually and if a new food is rejected don't try it again for a few days or, alternatively, combine it with baby rice or another type of purée.

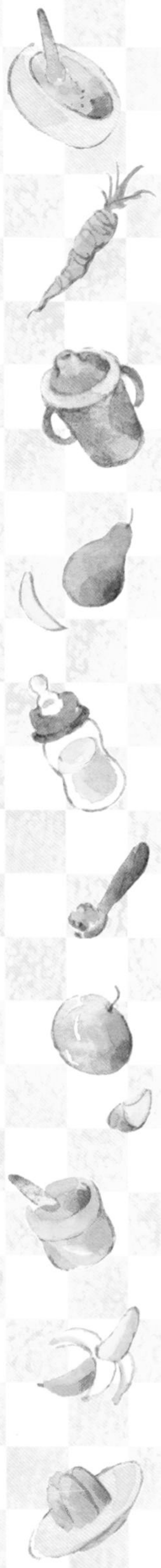

MEAL PLANNER 1

4 MONTHS	EARLY MORNING	BREAKFAST
WEEK 1		
Days 1–7	Milk	Milk
WEEK 2		
Days 1–4	Milk	Milk
Days 4–7	Milk	Milk
WEEK THREE		
Days 1–3	Milk	Banana purée, milk
Days 3–5	Milk	Apple purée, milk
Days 5–7	Milk	Pear purée, milk
WEEK FOUR		
Day 1	Milk	Apple purée, milk
Day 2	Milk	Apple purée, milk
Day 3	Milk	Baby rice, milk
Day 4	Milk	Baby rice, milk
Day 5	Milk	Pear purée, baby rice
Day 6	Milk	Pear purée, baby rice
Day 7	Milk	Banana purée, baby rice

5-6 MONTHS	EARLY MORNING	BREAKFAST
Day 1	Milk	Baby cereal, milk
Day 2	Milk	Mashed banana, milk
Day 3	Milk	Dried apricot purée, milk
Day 4	Milk	Pear purée, baby rice, milk
Day 5	Milk	Baby cereal, milk
Day 6	Milk	Apple purée, milk
Day 7	Milk	Mango purée, baby rice, milk

LUNCH	TEA	BEDTIME
Baby rice, milk	Milk	Milk
Apple purée, milk	Milk	Milk
Carrot purée, milk	Milk	Milk
Milk	Carrot purée, milk	Milk
Milk	Potato purée, milk	Milk
Milk	Sweet potato purée, milk	Milk
Courgette purée, milk	Sweet potato purée, milk	Milk
Courgette purée, milk	Carrot purée, milk	Milk
Banana purée, milk	Carrot purée, milk	Milk
Banana purée, milk	Potato purée, milk	Milk
Carrot purée, milk	Potato purée, milk	Milk
Carrot purée, milk	Apple purée, milk	Milk
Sweet potato purée, milk	Courgette purée, milk	Milk

LUNCH	TEA	BEDTIME
(with diluted unsweetened fruit juice – 1 part juice: 5 parts water)		
Cauliflower, potato & leek purée, apple purée	Mango purée, rice cake, milk	Milk
Avocado purée, rusk & milk	Apricot & swede purée	Milk
Broccoli & pea purée, melon purée	Apple & banana purée, milk	Milk
Avocado purée, apple purée	Orchard fruit purée, milk	Milk
Spinach & French bean purée, melon purée	Sweet potato & apple purée, rusk & milk	Milk
Cauliflower, potato & leek purée, mango purée	Dried apricot purée, rice cake, milk	Milk
Apple, parsnip & squash purée, pear purée	Broccoli & pea purée, rusk & milk	Milk

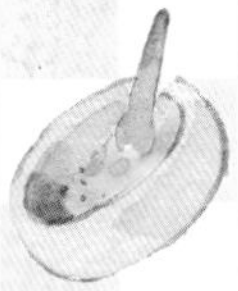

Baby Rice

PREPARATION TIME *3 minutes* **COOKING TIME** *20–25 minutes*

FREEZING *suitable* **MAKES** *15 portions*

Baby rice is a good introduction to solid foods and can be mixed with breast or formula milk to make a runny purée. There are many commercial versions of baby rice around but it is just as easy to make at home. Admittedly, home-made baby rice is not fortified with extra vitamins, but at this stage your baby should be getting all the nutrients needed from breast or formula milk.

1. Rinse the rice under cold running water. Put the rice into a saucepan and add enough cold water to just cover it. Bring to the boil, stir, then reduce the heat. Cover the pan and simmer for 20–25 minutes, until the water has been absorbed and the grains are very tender.

2. Purée the rice in a blender with breast or formula milk until smooth and creamy.

INGREDIENTS

40 g/1½ oz white short-grain rice

COOK'S TIP

Baby rice makes an ideal base for any fruit or vegetable purées and is a simple and easy way of introducing your baby to new tastes and textures. Apple or pear work particularly well with baby rice and are delicious with a sprinkling of ground cinnamon. If using frozen baby rice, make sure it has completely defrosted and is heated through thoroughly before using.

Fruit and Vegetable Purées

These basic fruit and vegetable purées make perfect first foods for your baby. I have intentionally kept them simple to enable him or her to become accustomed to eating solids and tasting new flavours. In time, the purées can be combined to make a wider choice of taste variations. The portion sizes given are a rough guide. You will find that your baby will eat no more than a few teaspoons at first – if that. Store the remainder in the fridge for use the next day or double up the quantity given and freeze.

Pear Purée

PREPARATION TIME *2 minutes* **COOKING TIME** *5–8 minutes*
FREEZING *suitable* **MAKES** *2–3 portions*

It is unnecessary to cook pears after your baby is 6 months old but, prior to this, cooking is advisable to make the fruit easier to digest.

1. Wash, peel, core and chop the pear. Put the pear into a saucepan with the water. Bring to the boil and cook for 5–8 minutes, until the fruit is tender.

2. Purée the pear in a blender until smooth, adding a little of the cooking water if necessary.

INGREDIENTS
1 small ripe pear
2 tbsp water

VARIATION

Apple can be cooked and puréed in the same way as pear for a digestible purée. Apple is often the most popular fruit!

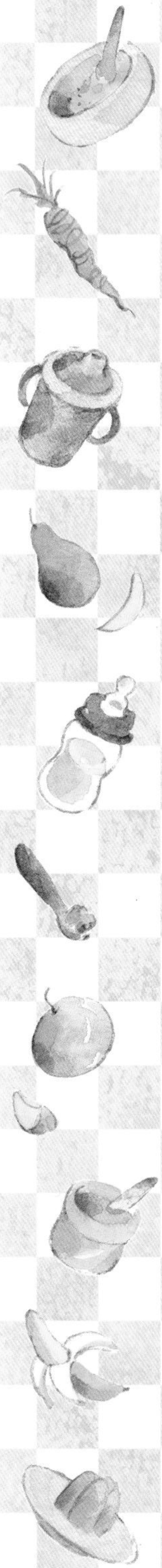

Carrot Purée

PREPARATION TIME *2 minutes* **COOKING TIME** *10–15 minutes*
FREEZING *suitable* **MAKES** *1–2 portions*

The natural sweetness of carrots makes this purée a popular first food. Pick small, young, preferably organic vegetables.

INGREDIENTS
1 small carrot
2 tbsp water

1. Scrape or peel the carrot, then slice. Put the carrot into a saucepan with the water. Bring to the boil and cook for 10–15 minutes, until tender.

2. Purée the carrot in a blender until smooth, adding a little of the cooking water if necessary.

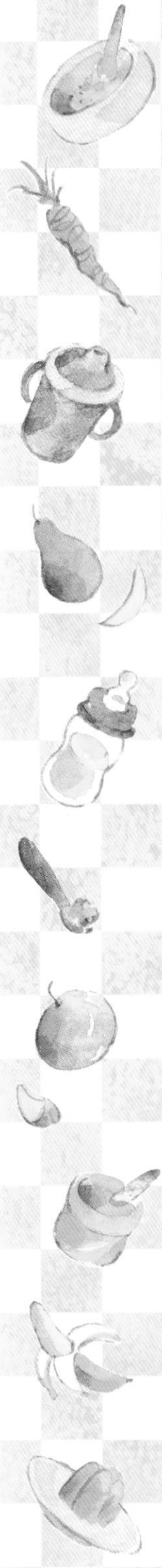

Courgette Purée

PREPARATION TIME *2 minutes* **COOKING TIME** *4–5 minutes*

FREEZING *suitable* **MAKES** *2 portions*

Courgette can be a difficult vegetable to introduce to your child, so it is best to offer it at as young an age as possible. It can be combined with potato to make it more palatable, if you wish.

❶ Trim and slice the courgette – there is no need to peel it. Steam or boil the courgette for 4–5 minutes, until tender.

❷ Purée in a blender until smooth or mash with a fork.

INGREDIENTS
1 medium courgette

VARIATION

Potato and sweet potato purées can be useful bases for other vegetables. Cut a whole potato in small cubes. Bring a pan of water to the boil and cook the potato for 15–20 minutes until tender. Purée with breast or formula milk until smooth and creamy.

Avocado Purée

PREPARATION TIME *2 minutes*

FREEZING *unsuitable* **MAKES** *1 portion*

Choose ripe, unblemished fruit for this purée and prepare just before serving because avocado flesh discolours very quickly after it has been cut.

❶ Peel and stone the avocado and scoop out the flesh with a spoon. Mash the avocado with a fork until smooth and creamy.

❷ Serve immediately before the flesh browns and discolours.

INGREDIENTS

½ small avocado

COOK'S TIP

Squeeze fresh lemon juice over the unused avocado half to prevent the flesh discolouring. The avocado can then be kept in the refrigerator for use the following day.

Mango Purée

PREPARATION TIME *2 minutes* **COOKING TIME** *2 minutes*
FREEZING *suitable* **MAKES** *2–3 portions*

Mangoes are loved by babies, as they are naturally sweet and easy to digest. They are also a good introduction to the more 'tropical' kinds of fruit available. Do make sure the mango is ripe before you use it – unripe fruit can upset small stomachs.

INGREDIENTS
1 small ripe mango

❶ Wash, peel, stone and slice the mango. Steam for 2 minutes or, if very ripe, mash with a fork or pass through a sieve until smooth to remove the fibres.

Melon Purée

PREPARATION TIME *2 minutes* **COOKING TIME** *2 minutes*

FREEZING *unsuitable* **MAKES** *1–2 portions*

Any variety of melon can be given uncooked to babies as long as it's sweet and juicy. It may be necessary to steam the fruit if it's not entirely ripe. Galia, Charentais and Cantaloupe melons tend to have the sweetest flesh.

❶ Peel the melon then remove any seeds before chopping it. Mash with a fork or pass through a sieve until smooth.

❷ Alternatively, steam for 2 minutes, until tender, and mash with a fork until smooth.

INGREDIENTS

1 wedge of melon

VARIATION

A banana can be mashed in the same way as melon for a tasty purée. Be sure to use ripe fruit.

Dried Apricot Purée

PREPARATION TIME *2 minutes* **COOKING TIME** *10–15 minutes*
FREEZING *suitable* **MAKES** *3–5 portions*

Dried apricots are a good source of iron and beta-carotene but must be soaked overnight to make them easier to eat. Like other dried fruits, apricots have a laxative effect so it's important that they are given in small amounts. Other dried fruit such as prunes, apples, pears and peaches make suitable alternatives.

INGREDIENTS

8 unsulphured, dried, ready-to-eat apricots

1. Wash and soak the apricots in cold water overnight. The next day, drain the apricots and place in a saucepan.

2. Cover with water and bring to the boil, then reduce the heat and simmer for 10–15 minutes, until soft. Purée in a blender until smooth, adding a little of the cooking water if necessary.

Orchard Fruit Purée

PREPARATION TIME *4 minutes* **COOKING TIME** *5 minutes*

FREEZING *suitable* **MAKES** *6–8 portions*

A firm favourite with little ones. It also makes a delicious accompaniment to roasts and vegetarian alternatives.

INGREDIENTS
1 small dessert apple
1 small ripe pear
1 small ripe peach

1. Wash, peel, core or stone the fruit, then chop into small pieces. Steam or boil the apple and pear for 5 minutes, or until soft.

2. Purée the apple and pear with the peach in a blender until smooth, adding a little of the cooking water if necessary.

Broccoli & Pea Purée

PREPARATION TIME *2 minutes* **COOKING TIME** *5–6 minutes*

FREEZING *suitable* **MAKES** *2–3 portions*

A vibrant combination that is full of goodness. This bright green purée is certainly a colourful dish!

INGREDIENTS
3 florets broccoli
handful of frozen peas

❶ Steam or boil the broccoli for 5–6 minutes, adding the peas 5 minutes before the end of the cooking time.

❷ Purée the broccoli and peas in a blender until smooth, adding a little of the cooking water if necessary.

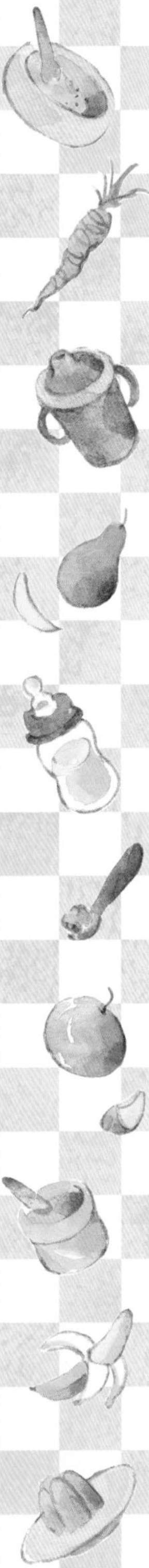

Cauliflower, Potato & Leek Purée

PREPARATION TIME *3 minutes* **COOKING TIME** *15–20 minutes*

FREEZING *suitable* **MAKES** *4–6 portions*

Introducing potential 'problem' vegetables at an early age can cut down on fussy eating when your child gets older. This combination also works well with broccoli and sweet potato.

INGREDIENTS
1 medium potato
3 florets cauliflower
½ small leek

1. Wash, peel and cube the potato. Wash the leek, remove the tough outer layer, then slice thinly. Steam or boil the potato, cauliflower and leek for 15–20 minutes, until tender.

2. Purée in a blender with a little breast or formula milk until smooth and creamy.

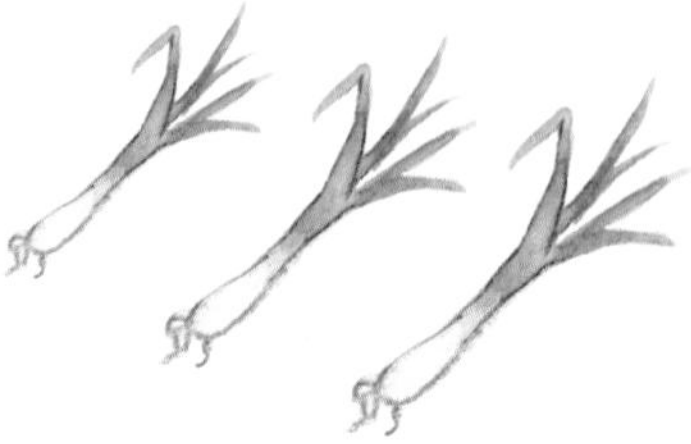

Apricot & Swede Purée

PREPARATION TIME *3 minutes* **COOKING TIME** *15–20 minutes*
FREEZING *suitable* **MAKES** *2–3 portions*

It is a good idea to encourage your baby to try a range of fruit and vegetable combinations in the hope that your child will not be a fussy eater in the future – well, that's the theory!

INGREDIENTS
1 wedge of swede
2 fresh ripe apricots

❶ Wash, peel and cube the wedge of swede. Halve the apricots and then stone them carefully. Steam or boil the swede for 15–20 minutes until tender, adding the apricots 5 minutes before the end of the cooking time.

❷ Sieve to remove the apricot skin and purée in a blender until smooth, adding a little of the cooking water if necessary.

Spinach & French Bean Purée

PREPARATION TIME *3 minutes* **COOKING TIME** *8 minutes*

FREEZING *suitable* **MAKES** *3–4 portions*

From around 6 months of age, your baby's natural iron stores begin to deplete and it is vital at this stage to introduce foods that provide this mineral. Spinach is a good source of iron, which is more readily absorbed if it is served with a cup of very dilute fresh orange juice.

INGREDIENTS
3 French beans
40 g/1½ oz fresh young spinach leaves

1. Wash, trim and slice the beans. Wash the spinach and remove any coarse stalks. Steam or boil the beans for 8 minutes. Steam the spinach for 5 minutes, until tender and wilted, then squeeze out any excess water.

2. Purée in a blender until smooth, adding a little of the cooking water if necessary.

Apple, Parsnip & Butternut Squash Purée

PREPARATION TIME *3 minutes* **COOKING TIME** *15 minutes*

FREEZING *suitable* **MAKES** *3–4 portions*

Butternut squash is a good source of vitamin C and, when puréed, makes a nourishing meal.

❶ Wash, peel and dice the parsnip and squash. Wash, peel, core and chop the apple. Place the parsnip and squash in a saucepan and cover with water. Bring to the boil and cook for 15 minutes until tender, adding the apple 5 minutes before the end of the cooking time.

INGREDIENTS
1 small parsnip
1 small wedge of butternut squash
1 small dessert apple

❷ Purée the apple, parsnip and butternut squash in a blender until smooth, adding a little of the cooking water if necessary.

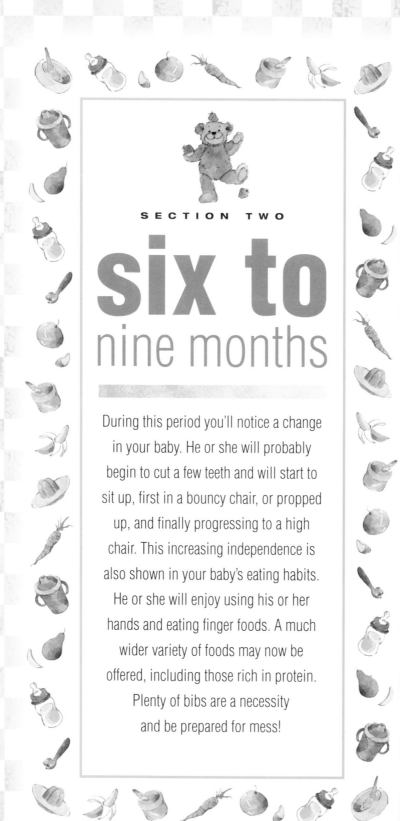

SECTION TWO

six to nine months

During this period you'll notice a change in your baby. He or she will probably begin to cut a few teeth and will start to sit up, first in a bouncy chair, or propped up, and finally progressing to a high chair. This increasing independence is also shown in your baby's eating habits. He or she will enjoy using his or her hands and eating finger foods. A much wider variety of foods may now be offered, including those rich in protein. Plenty of bibs are a necessity and be prepared for mess!

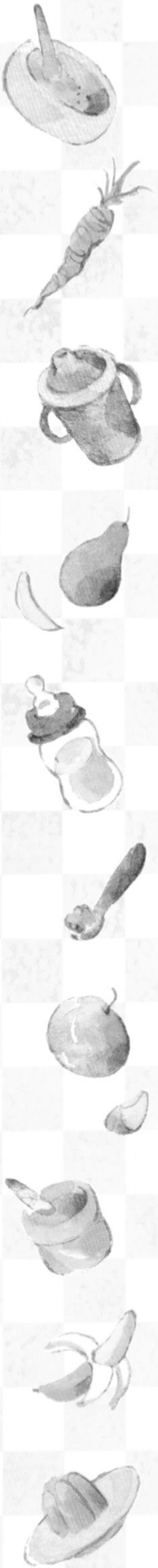

New Tastes & Textures

Once your baby is happy with his or her first foods, it is time to introduce a wider range of fruits and vegetables, as well as protein foods such as lean meat, white fish, cottage cheese, yogurt and well-cooked eggs. Health practitioners call this the second stage of weaning.

NEW TASTES

Although milk will still form an important part of your baby's diet, it no longer provides all the necessary nutrients. If your baby is happily taking solids, you'll probably find that he or she can now eat many family meals, but avoid highly spiced or seasoned foods. It is a good idea to remove a baby-sized portion of what you are eating before seasoning the remainder of the meal.

At this stage, it's a good idea to familiarise your baby with a wider range of flavours and you will definitely reap the benefits in the future. Many nutritionists recommend that lentils, beans, chicken and fish be given after eight months but take extra care to remove any hidden bones in fish. These foods combine well with other foods, especially those with stronger flavours, have a pleasing texture and take little time to prepare. Mash beans and lentils well and only use in small quantities, since they can be difficult to digest. Fromage frais and yogurt lend themselves to many types of dishes and add a delicious creaminess to pasta sauces, soups and stews. Eggs must be well cooked and mashed or finely chopped to avoid choking. Some health practitioners recommend giving only the yolk between six to eight months as the egg white can be difficult to digest. Pasta and bread are great favourites with children and are versatile.

From six months, your baby's iron stores start to deplete, so it is important to include sources of iron (see page 7) in his or her diet. Vitamin C-rich foods and drinks can enhance the iron absorption and it is a good idea to offer them at the same time.

Babies love fruit – citrus fruit, strawberries and mango can now be included, although it is wise to limit the quantities as they can be acidic on the stomach.

THREE MEALS A DAY

There are no hard and fast rules when it comes to how much your

ABOVE *Fresh fruit is a great favourite with babies – the larger and juicier the better!*

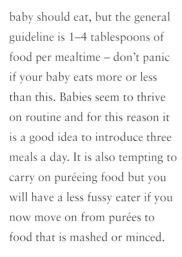

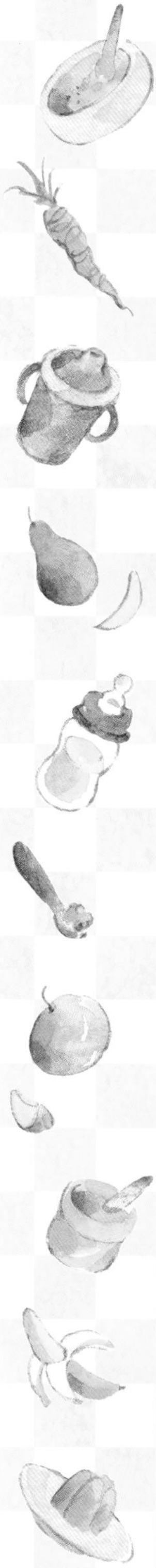

baby should eat, but the general guideline is 1–4 tablespoons of food per mealtime – don't panic if your baby eats more or less than this. Babies seem to thrive on routine and for this reason it is a good idea to introduce three meals a day. It is also tempting to carry on puréeing food but you will have a less fussy eater if you now move on from purées to food that is mashed or minced.

MILK AND DRINKS

You'll find that as your baby's appetite increases, his or her need for milk will decline. He or she should still be drinking 600 ml/1 pint of breast, formula or follow-on milk each day, but once solid feeding is established, it is advisable to stop giving milk at mealtimes because it can depress the appetite, as well as interfere with the absorption of certain minerals. Avoid giving cow's milk as a drink, although it is now suitable for cooking. Instead, give cooled boiled water or very weak unsweetened fruit juice.

FINGER FOODS

Fingers foods help to comfort sore gums and also give your baby a chance to use his or her hands and practise chewing. Lightly steamed sticks of carrot, baby sweetcorn, mangetout and pepper are popular, as are peeled chunks of apple, pear, banana, melon and papaya. Fingers of pitta bread, rusks and breadsticks are also ideal for new textures.

MEAL PLANNER 2

6-9 MONTHS	EARLY MORNING	BREAKFAST	SLEEP
		(with diluted unsweetened fruit juice – 1 part juice: 5 parts water – or cooled boiled water)	
Day 1	Milk	Apricot porridge	Milk
Day 2	Milk	Weetabix & banana purée	Milk
Day 3	Milk	Fromage frais & mango purée Toast fingers	Milk
Day 4	Milk	Ready Brek & pear purée	Milk
Day 5	Milk	Apricot porridge	Milk
Day 6	Milk	Baby cereal & pear purée	Milk
Day 7	Milk	Weetabix & banana purée	Milk

Note If your baby is under 8 months, substitute the tuna salad with pastina on day 3; spring vegetable risotto for the chicken and pineapple cheese on day 4; and leave out the plaice in the baked plaice with tomato rice on day 5.

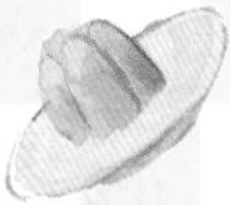

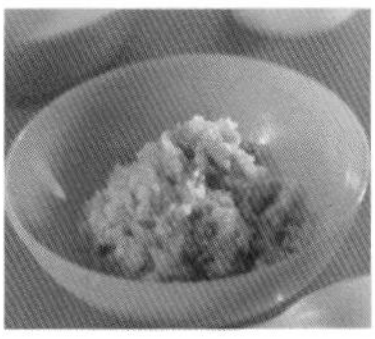

LUNCH	SLEEP	TEA	BEDTIME
(same drink as breakfast)		(same drink as lunch)	
Carrot, bean & swede purée Pear purée	Milk	Avocado purée & toast fingers Banana yogurt custard	Milk
Spring vegetable risotto Fromage frais & mango purée	Milk	Houmus with crudités Pitta bread Apricot porridge	Milk
Cauliflower, potato & leek purée Sunset jelly	Milk	Tuna salad Apple & plum yogurt	Milk
Apple, parsnip & butternut squash purée Fromage frais & apricot purée	Milk	Chicken & pineapple cheese Breadsticks Sunset jelly	Milk
Baked plaice with tomato rice Pear purée	Milk	Pastina Banana yogurt custard	Milk
Oaty vegetable purée Melon purée	Milk	Bean & root vegetable mash Fromage frais & mango purée	Milk
Minestrone soup Toast fingers Orchard fruit purée	Milk	Tuna salad Apple & plum yogurt	Milk

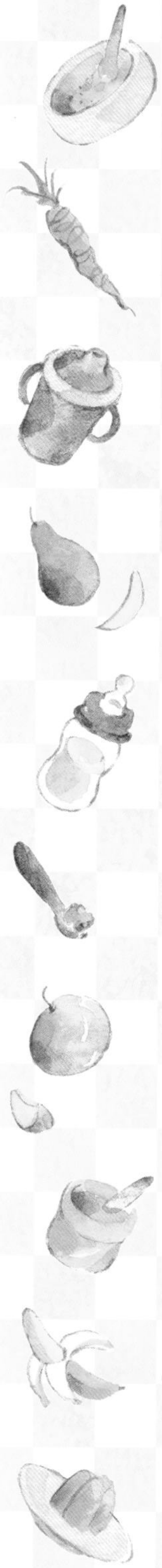

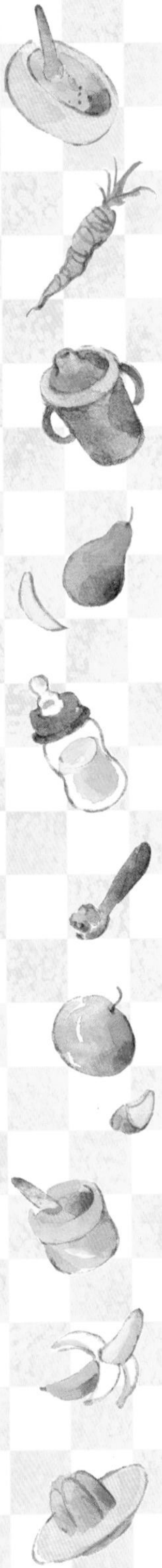

Oaty Vegetable Purée

PREPARATION TIME *5 minutes* **COOKING TIME** *20 minutes*

FREEZING *suitable* **MAKES** *4–6 portions*

The addition of oats to this wholesome purée means there is plenty of substance – something for your baby to use new teeth on! This purée also introduces tomato to your child's diet.

INGREDIENTS
2 tbsp porridge oats
1 small leek, finely chopped
2 tbsp canned sweetcorn, drained and rinsed
1 medium tomato, skinned, seeded and chopped
small knob of unsalted butter or margarine

1. Put the oats into a saucepan, cover with half water and half milk and bring to the boil. Reduce the heat and simmer, stirring occasionally, for 4–5 minutes, until the grains are soft and creamy.

2. Meanwhile, steam the leek for 10–15 minutes, until tender. Combine the leek with the oats, sweetcorn, tomato and butter in a small saucepan and stir until heated through. Purée or mash, depending on the desired consistency. (You may need to add a little extra breast, formula or cow's milk.)

VARIATION

Carrot, French bean and swede cooked and puréed is a tasty combination.

Minestrone Soup

PREPARATION TIME *10 minutes* **COOKING TIME** *35 minutes*
FREEZING *suitable* **MAKES** *4 portions*

This classic Italian soup is a nutritious combination of beans, pasta and vegetables, providing a good range of vitamins and minerals.

INGREDIENTS
1 tbsp olive oil
½ small onion, finely chopped
1 small carrot, peeled and diced
1 bay leaf
300 ml/½ pint no-salt or low-salt vegetable stock
4 tbsp passata
55 g/2 oz small pasta shapes
4 tbsp canned, no-salt, no-sugar haricot beans, drained and rinsed
25 g/1 oz spinach, washed and thick stalks removed, finely chopped
2 tbsp freshly grated Parmesan cheese

❶ Heat the olive oil in a heavy-based saucepan. Add the onion and carrot and cook over a medium heat for 8–10 minutes, stirring occasionally, until the vegetables have softened.

❷ Add the bay leaf, stock and passata, then bring to the boil. Reduce the heat, cover, and simmer for 15 minutes, or until the vegetables are tender.

❸ Add the pasta and beans, then bring the soup back to the boil and simmer until the pasta is tender. Stir occasionally to prevent the pasta sticking.

❹ Add the spinach and cook for a further 2 minutes, or until the spinach is tender. Stir in the Parmesan cheese and purée, mash or chop the mixture, depending on the age of your baby.

Spring Vegetable Risotto

PREPARATION TIME *5 minutes* **COOKING TIME** *35–40 minutes*
FREEZING *suitable* **MAKES** *6–8 portions*

Rice is perfect for babies as it is comforting and easy to eat. I have used spring vegetables here but do experiment with others.

INGREDIENTS
1 small leek, peeled and finely chopped
1 small courgette, finely chopped
small handful of frozen peas
1 tsp olive oil
small knob of unsalted butter
85 g/3 oz arborio rice
350 ml/12 fl oz hot no-salt or low-salt vegetable or chicken stock
½ tsp dried oregano
2 tbsp freshly grated Parmesan cheese

❶ Steam the leek and courgette for 5–8 minutes, until tender.

❷ Heat the oil and butter in a heavy-based saucepan. When the butter has melted, add the rice and stir for a couple of minutes until it is coated with the oil and has become translucent.

❸ Add the stock a ladleful at a time, waiting until it has been absorbed before adding more. Bring to the boil and simmer for 20 minutes, stirring continuously. Add the oregano, Parmesan and vegetables and simmer, stirring, for a further 5–10 minutes, until the liquid has been absorbed and the rice is tender. Purée the risotto for younger babies, adding extra stock or water if it is too thick.

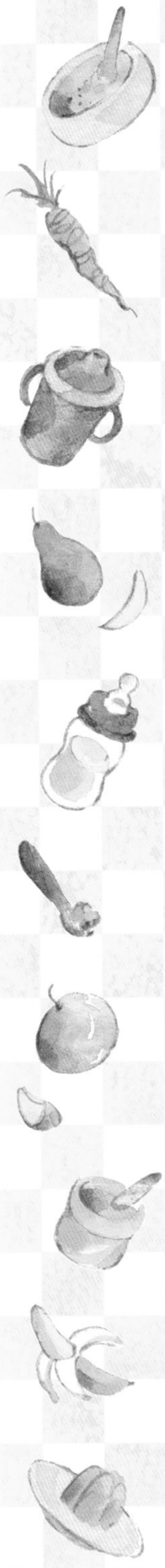

Baked Plaice with Tomato Rice

PREPARATION TIME *10 minutes* **COOKING TIME** *30 minutes*

FREEZING *suitable* **MAKES** *6–8 portions*

It is not advisable to give fish to babies before they are 8 months old but, in this case, the tomato rice is as good served on its own.

INGREDIENTS
1 small plaice fillet
olive oil, for brushing
2 medium tomatoes, skinned, seeded and coarsely chopped
85 g/3 oz brown long-grain rice, washed
4 tbsp canned chopped tomatoes
175 ml/6 fl oz water
1 sprig of fresh basil leaves
½ tsp dried oregano
1 small carrot, peeled and diced
3 fine French beans, sliced

1. Preheat the oven to 350°F/180°C/Gas Mark 4. Put the plaice on a large piece of baking paper, brush it with oil and arrange the fresh tomatoes on top. Fold up the baking paper to make a parcel and encase the fish. Place the parcel on a baking sheet and bake for 20 minutes.

2. Put the rice and chopped tomatoes in a saucepan and cover with the water. Bring to the boil and add the sprig of basil, oregano, carrot and beans. Reduce the heat, cover, and simmer for 20 minutes, until the water has been absorbed and the rice, carrot and beans are tender.

3. Remove the basil sprig. Carefully remove the skin and any bones from the fish and flake the flesh. Fold the fish and fresh tomatoes into the tomato rice and serve puréed or mashed.

Chicken & Pineapple Cheese

PREPARATION TIME *10 minutes* **COOKING TIME** *15 minutes*
FREEZING *unsuitable* **MAKES** *2 portions*

This couldn't be more simple or quick to make but, due to the inclusion of cottage cheese, it is best reserved for babies from 8 months old. Serve it mashed with fingers of toast or pitta bread, or blend to make a nutritious sandwich filling.

INGREDIENTS
1 tsp olive oil
55 g/2 oz skinless chicken breast, chopped
4 tbsp cottage cheese
1 tbsp natural yogurt
1 slice of fresh pineapple, cored and diced

❶ Heat the oil in a non-stick frying pan. Add the chicken breast and cook for 12–15 minutes, turning occasionally, until tender and lightly browned. Set aside to cool slightly. Finely chop the chicken.

❷ Combine the chicken with the cottage cheese, yogurt and pineapple and mash together. Alternatively, for younger babies, place all the ingredients in a blender and blend the mixture to a coarse purée.

Pastina with Butternut Squash

PREPARATION TIME *5 minutes* **COOKING TIME** *15 minutes*

FREEZING *suitable* **MAKES** *4–6 portions*

This nurturing dish is a favourite weaning food in Italy.

❶ Steam the butternut squash for 10–15 minutes, until tender, and purée or mash with a fork.

❷ Meanwhile, cook the pasta according to the instructions on the packet, until it is tender. Add the butter, oil and Parmesan cheese and stir until the pasta is coated, then combine with the butternut squash.

INGREDIENTS
85 g/3 oz butternut squash, peeled, seeded and chopped
85 g/3 oz baby pasta shapes or soup pasta (pastina)
small knob of unsalted butter
1 tsp olive oil
2 tbsp freshly grated Parmesan cheese

Tuna Salad

PREPARATION TIME *5 minutes*

FREEZING *unsuitable* **MAKES** *4–6 portions*

Babies from 8 months can enjoy this first introduction to salad. It works well as a dip with breadsticks, pitta bread and sticks of raw or lightly steamed carrot, baby sweetcorn, red pepper, cucumber and apple, or spread over rice cakes or bread.

1. Place the tuna, avocado, cottage cheese, yogurt, tomato, chives and lemon juice in a bowl and mash until combined and smooth or to the desired consistency.

INGREDIENTS
2 tbsp canned tuna in oil, drained and mashed
½ avocado, peeled, stoned and chopped
4 tbsp cottage cheese
1 tbsp natural yogurt
1 medium tomato, skinned, seeded and finely chopped
1 tsp finely chopped fresh chives
squeeze of fresh lemon juice

Bean & Root Vegetable Mash

PREPARATION TIME *5 minutes* **COOKING TIME** *20 minutes*

FREEZING *suitable* **MAKES** *4 portions*

This comforting combination is a favourite with little ones and adults alike. For young babies, the beans should be mashed or puréed until smooth.

❶ Cook the potato and swede in boiling water for 15–20 minutes, until tender. Drain and purée or mash with the olive oil and butter.

❷ Heat the beans through and mash or chop, depending on the age of your baby. Peel the egg and discard the white. Mash the egg yolk and combine with the beans and mashed potato.

INGREDIENTS
1 medium potato, peeled and cubed
85 g/3 oz swede or celeriac, peeled and cubed
1 tsp olive oil
small knob of unsalted butter or margarine
4 tbsp no-salt, no-sugar baked beans
1 hard-boiled egg yolk

Houmus with Crudités

PREPARATION TIME *10 minutes*

FREEZING *unsuitable* **MAKES** *10 portions*

Houmus not only makes a nutritious, convenient snack, but a spoonful stirred into a soup or sauce can also add substance and flavour. Choose from the selection of crudités mentioned below, but for young babies the vegetables should be steamed to make them easier to eat. Apple, pear and peach are also delicious.

INGREDIENTS
200 g/7 oz no-salt, no-sugar canned chickpeas, drained and rinsed
½ clove garlic, crushed
3 tbsp tahini (sesame seed paste)
freshly squeezed lemon juice, to taste
1 tbsp natural yogurt

❶ Place the chickpeas in a blender with the garlic, tahini, lemon juice and yogurt. Blend to a smooth purée.

❷ Store covered in the refrigerator for up to 3 days and serve with the crudités, which can be steamed or raw.

❸ The following fruits and vegetables can be used as crudités: slices of apple, pear and peach; sticks of carrot, French beans, red pepper, baby sweetcorn and mangetout.

Apricot Porridge

PREPARATION TIME *10 minutes* **COOKING TIME** *15 minutes*

FREEZING *suitable* **MAKES** *4 portions*

Most of the following desserts can double up as a breakfast, which is worth remembering if you have plenty left over. The dried apricots are cooked and puréed and are delicious with yogurt or fromage frais. Dates make a delicious alternative.

INGREDIENTS
6 unsulphured dried, ready-to-eat apricots
8 tbsp porridge oats

❶ Wash and soak the apricots in cold water overnight. The next day, drain the apricots and place in a saucepan. Cover with water and bring to the boil, then reduce the heat and simmer for 10–15 minutes, until soft.

❷ Purée the cooked apricots in a blender until smooth, adding a little of the cooking water if necessary.

❸ Meanwhile, cover the oats with half water and half milk. Bring to the boil, reduce the heat and simmer for 5–8 minutes, until the oats are tender and creamy. Combine with some or all of the apricot purée.

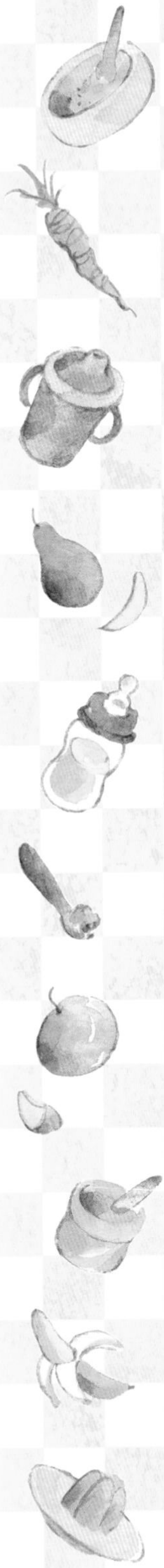

Banana Yogurt Custard

PREPARATION TIME *5 minutes*

FREEZING *unsuitable* **MAKES** *2 portions*

Bananas, when they are well-ripened, are easy for your baby to digest and can be mashed into a smooth paste. This pudding is a good way of introducing yogurt into your child's diet, and it is more exciting when blended with the banana and custard.

1 Combine the mashed banana with the yogurt, custard and vanilla essence and mix well.

INGREDIENTS
1 small banana, mashed
2 tbsp Greek-style yogurt
2 tbsp made-up custard
few drops of vanilla essence

Fromage Frais & Mango Purée

PREPARATION TIME *5 minutes* **COOKING TIME** *2 minutes*

FREEZING *unsuitable* **MAKES** *2 portions*

Any of the fruit purées mentioned earlier can replace the mango in this recipe. The wheatgerm is a good source of fibre, vitamins and minerals but it can be left out if preferred.

❶ Steam the mango for 2 minutes or, if very ripe, mash with a fork and pass through a sieve until smooth. Mix well with the fromage frais and wheatgerm.

INGREDIENTS
½ small ripe mango, peeled and chopped
4–6 tbsp fromage frais
1 tsp wheatgerm

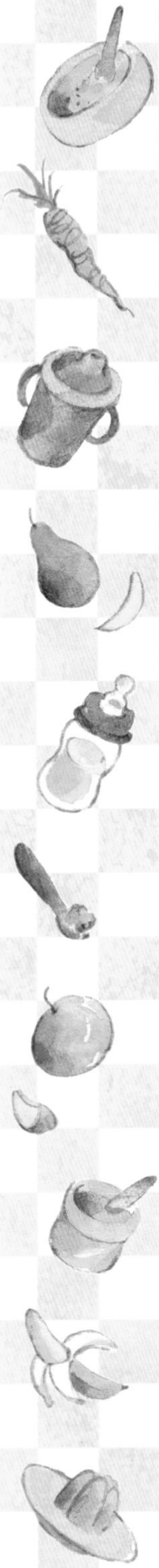

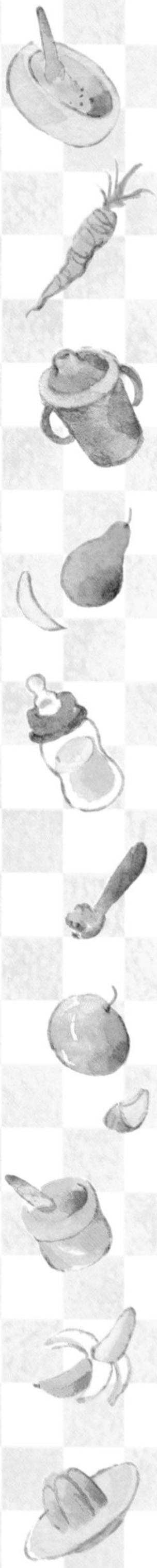

Apple & Plum Yogurt

PREPARATION TIME *5 minutes* **COOKING TIME** *5 minutes*

FREEZING *unsuitable* **MAKES** *2 portions*

Babies can dislike the texture of plums, so mixing them with apple and yogurt is a good idea to make them more baby friendly.

INGREDIENTS
2 tbsp water
1 small dessert apple, peeled, cored and chopped
2 ripe plums, stoned
4–6 tbsp natural yogurt
1 plain biscuit, crushed

❶ Put the apple and plums into a saucepan with the water. Bring to the boil and cook for 5 minutes, until tender. Remove the plum skins and purée in a blender or pass through a sieve until smooth.

❷ Mix together the fruit purée and yogurt and sprinkle over the crushed biscuit before serving.

Sunset Jelly

PREPARATION TIME *15 minutes, plus setting*

FREEZING *unsuitable* **MAKES** *4 portions*

Cubes of jelly are interspersed with pieces of fruit in this vibrant pudding. The yogurt provides a good source of calcium.

INGREDIENTS
½ pack of red jelly (raspberry, strawberry or cherry)
250 ml/8 fl oz boiling water
1 tbsp peach yogurt
1 slice of Galia melon, cubed
1 small ripe peach, peeled, stoned and cubed

1. Make the jelly as instructed on the packet, using the water. Whisk in the yogurt and allow to cool, then refrigerate until set.

2. Cut the jelly into cubes, dipping the knife into warm water to prevent it sticking. Arrange in a bowl with the melon and peach.

SECTION THREE

nine to twelve months

This can be a challenging but rewarding stage in a baby's development. There will be fewer occasions when a specially prepared meal is required, and he or she may start to enjoy the social aspect of eating with the family. At this stage, babies will also begin to exercise their desire for independence and a growing curiosity for what's around them. This can prove an interesting time, and plenty of patience and a sense of humour are the key to preserving your sanity!

Eating with the Family

Health practitioners refer to this period as the third stage of weaning, when most babies are accustomed to chewing small pieces of food and are able to join in most family meals. Your baby will now be sitting in a high chair and will probably have a few teeth, but may also become more fussy about what he or she eats.

NEW TASTES

Although you still have to restrict you baby's food salt intake and avoid whole nuts, shellfish and raw eggs, almost anything else goes. You may find that your baby rejects particular foods but it's essential not to make an issue of this. Your baby is unlikely to love everything that is presented before him or her and teething and general well-being can influence likes and dislikes on an almost daily basis. Try to offer the food again at a later stage.

The term 'balanced diet' can instil fear in most of us, but as long as your baby is eating a good mix of foods, including breads and cereals, lean meat and poultry, dairy products, beans and lentils and plenty of fruit and vegetables, then you are providing a range of nutrients.

As mentioned before, ensure your baby is eating sufficient amounts of iron-rich food (see page 7). This mineral is essential for good health and a deficiency can lead to irritability, anaemia and a poor immune system.

THREE MEALS A DAY

Babies seem to thrive on routine and because their stomachs are small they require three meals, plus a couple of snacks a day. The following menu also gives suggestions for light suppers but you may feel this is unnecessary. Ideally, and if convenient, the main meal of the day should be lunch. Babies seem to be more open to new tastes at this time of day, when they are alert and less fractious – the same can be said of parents! It also allows the digestive system to cope with unfamiliar new foods. At this stage baby foods don't need to be puréed. Coarsely mashed, grated and chopped foods will help your child's teeth and allow them to practise their chewing skills.

Good hygiene practices are paramount but it is now

unnecessary to sterilise every eating utensil that your baby uses. This is with the exception of bottles and teats, which are difficult to clean and can be a breeding ground for germs.

MILK AND DRINKS

Milk remains an important source of nutrients and your baby still requires about 600 ml/ 1 pint a day, although some of this can be provided by milky puddings and sauces and in breakfast cereals. Avoid giving cow's milk as a drink, opting for breast, formula or follow-on milk instead. Offer water or unsweetened fruit juice, 1 part juice to 5 parts water, at mealtimes in a cup or beaker.

FINGER FOODS

Finger foods can offer some relief to babies who are teething. Lightly steamed sticks of vegetables or peeled raw fruit are ideal for helping sore gums, especially if they are chilled. Fingers of bread, slowly dried in the oven, are a healthy alternative to commercial baby rusks, which can contain added sugar and other undesirable ingredients. Fingers of pitta, chapatti, muffins or naan bread can be dipped into houmus or vegetable purées, but make sure you never leave a baby unattended while eating because of possible choking.

BELOW *It is a good feeling when your baby is able to join in with the family meal and enjoy it!*

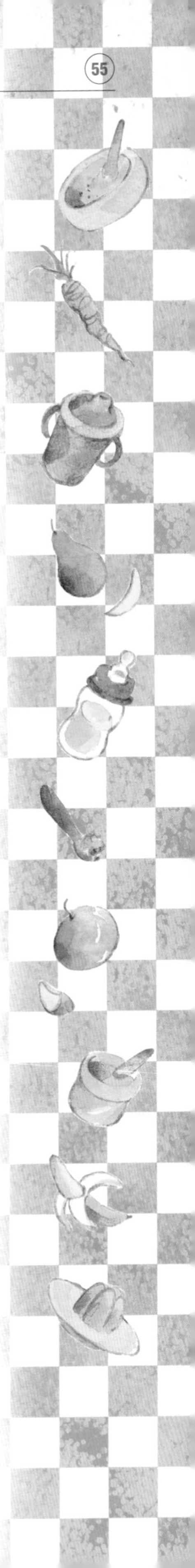

MEAL PLANNER 3

9-12 MONTHS	BREAKFAST	MID-MORNING
Day 1	Coconut muesli Toast & milk	Milk
Day 2	Well-cooked scrambled egg Grilled tomatoes Toast & milk	Milk
Day 3	Weetabix & banana Muffin & milk	Milk
Day 4	Apricot porridge Milk & toast	Milk
Day 5	Ready Brek Fruit bread Milk	Milk
Day 6	Coconut muesli Toast & milk	Milk
Day 7	Well-cooked poached egg Toasted muffin Milk	Milk

LUNCH	TEA	SUPPER	BEDTIME
(with diluted unsweetened fruit juice – 1 part juice: 5 parts water – or cooled boiled water)	(same drink as lunch)	(same drink as tea)	
Herby pasta cheese Banana cinnamon toast	Tuna salad New potatoes Fromage frais	Green fingers Tortilla/pitta bread Fruit	Milk
Moroccan couscous Baked apple crumblies	Muffin pizzas Houmus & crudités Banana yogurt custard	Pastina Vegetable fingers Fruit	Milk
Baked plaice with tomato rice Sunny honey sundae	Bean & root vegetable mash Apple & plum yogurt	Sandwich Fruit	Milk
Chinese rice with omelette strips Banana cinnamon toast	Pink pasta salad Baked potato Ice cream	Houmus & crudités Pitta bread Fruit	Milk
Chicken & pineapple cheese Garlic bread Baked apple crumblies	Pastina Broccoli Fromage frais	Sandwich Fruit	Milk
Mini meatballs Sunny honey sundae	Minestrone soup Chocolate cinnamon rice pudding	Cheese on toast Fruit	Milk
Creamy salmon & broccoli pasta Sunset jelly	Spring vegetable risotto Banana & custard	Green fingers Tortilla/pitta bread Fruit	Milk

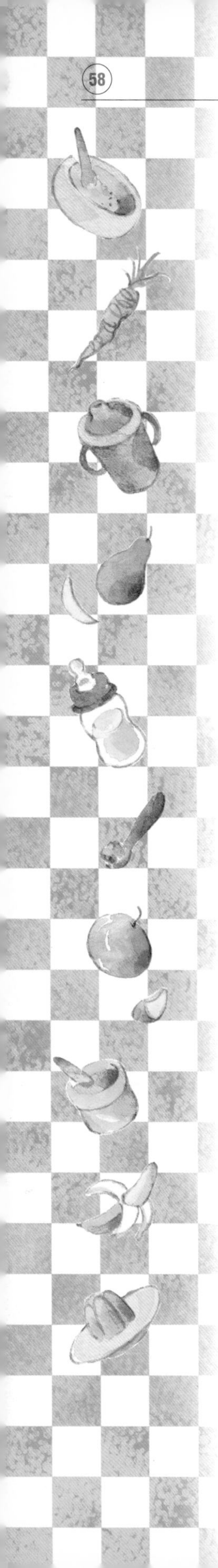

Chinese Rice with Omelette Strips

PREPARATION TIME *10 minutes* **COOKING TIME** *10 minutes*

FREEZING *suitable, if the rice has not been frozen before. Make the omelette just before serving*

MAKES *2 portions*

This is a great way of using up leftover cooked rice and surplus vegetables. Make sure you use cold rice and reheat it thoroughly before serving. Soy sauce is very salty, so just a splash should suffice in this dish.

INGREDIENTS
2 tsp vegetable oil
few drops of sesame oil
1 small clove garlic, finely chopped
pinch of Chinese five spice
1 carrot, peeled and diced
2 baby sweetcorn, halved and thinly sliced
2 tbsp water
small handful of baby spinach, tough stems removed and finely sliced
175 g/6 oz cooked, cold brown or white rice
dash of soy sauce
1 tsp sesame seeds, optional
small knob of unsalted butter
1 egg, beaten

❶ Heat the vegetable oil and sesame oil in a wok or heavy-based frying pan. Add the garlic, five spice, carrot and sweetcorn and stir-fry for 5 minutes, stirring and tossing continuously to prevent the spices and vegetables burning and sticking.

❷ Add the water and stir-fry for 2 minutes, then mix in the spinach and cook, stirring frequently, for a further 2 minutes, or until the vegetables are tender.

❸ Add the rice and a splash of soy sauce to the wok or pan and heat through thoroughly. Mix in the sesame seeds, if using.

❹ Meanwhile, melt the butter in a small heavy-based frying pan and add the egg. Swirl the egg until it covers the base of the pan. Cook until the egg has set and is cooked through, then turn out onto a plate. Cut the omelette into strips or small pieces.

❺ Place the rice in a bowl and arrange the omelette in a criss-cross pattern on top.

Herby Vegetable & Pasta Cheese

PREPARATION TIME *10 minutes* **COOKING TIME** *15 minutes*

FREEZING *suitable* **MAKES** *4–6 portions*

Although I've used broccoli and cauliflower here, this creamy cheese sauce goes well with many vegetables, especially carrot, swede, spinach and leeks. You could also try it with white fish. At this stage, it's fine to use cow's milk in moderation in cooking.

INGREDIENTS
4 florets broccoli, cut into small florets
4 florets cauliflower, cut into small florets
85 g/3 oz small penne or farfalle pasta
CHEESE SAUCE
1½ tbsp unsalted butter or margarine
1 tbsp plain flour
175 ml/6 fl oz full cream milk
½ tsp dried oregano
55 g/2 oz Cheddar cheese, grated

1. Steam the broccoli and cauliflower for 8–10 minutes, until tender. Cook the pasta according to the instructions on the packet, until the pasta is tender, then drain.

2. Meanwhile, make the cheese sauce. Melt the butter in a small heavy-based saucepan over a low heat. Gradually add the flour, beating well to form a smooth paste. Cook for 30 seconds, stirring continuously. Add the milk, a little at a time, whisking well to prevent any lumps forming, then stir in the oregano. Simmer for 2 minutes until smooth and creamy, then mix in the cheese. Stir until melted.

3. Add the cooked cauliflower, broccoli and pasta to the cheese sauce and stir well. Finely chop or mash the mixture.

Creamy Salmon & Broccoli Pasta

PREPARATION TIME *10 minutes* **COOKING TIME** *15 minutes*
FREEZING *unsuitable* **MAKES** *2–4 portions*

This delicious combination of cream cheese, salmon and broccoli is an excellent introduction to the health benefits of oily fish.

INGREDIENTS
85 g/3 oz small pasta shells
55 g/2 oz broccoli florets
1 tsp oil
small knob of unsalted butter
1 small leek, finely chopped
140 g/5 oz salmon fillet, skin and bones removed, cubed
4 tbsp garlic and herb cream cheese
2–3 tbsp full cream milk

1. Cook the pasta according to the instructions on the packet, until tender, then drain. Steam the broccoli for 8–10 minutes, until tender.

2. At the same time, prepare the sauce. Heat the oil and butter in a small heavy-based frying pan, then add the leek and cook for 7 minutes, or until softened. Add the salmon and cook for 2 minutes, or until just cooked and opaque. Stir in the cream cheese and milk and heat through.

3. Combine the sauce with the pasta and broccoli. Chop or mash the mixture finely to the desired consistency.

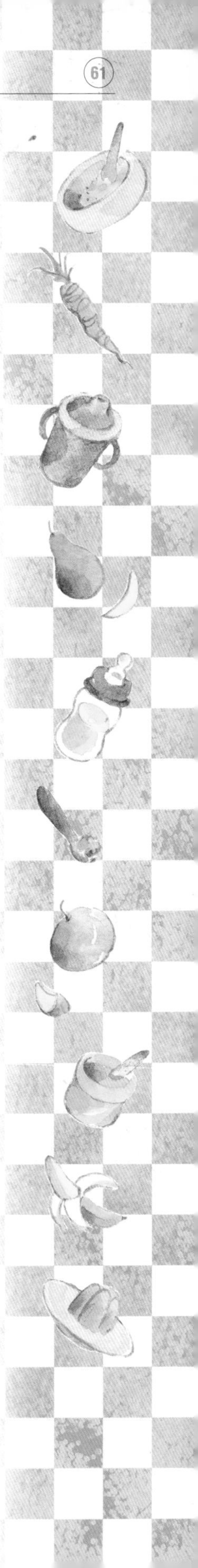

Moroccan Chicken Couscous

PREPARATION TIME *10 minutes* **COOKING TIME** *15 minutes*
FREEZING *unsuitable* **MAKES** *2 portions*

This recipe may sound exotic but it really is very easy to make and features just a hint of spice. Likes and dislikes develop at an early age so now is the time to encourage diverse tastes.

INGREDIENTS
55 g/2 oz couscous
small knob of unsalted butter
3 tsp olive oil
1 small onion, finely chopped
1 small skinless chicken breast, cut into bite-sized pieces
1 small clove garlic, finely chopped
½ tsp ground cumin
pinch of ground coriander
1 small peach or nectarine, stoned and diced
4 whole toasted almonds, finely chopped

❶ Place the couscous in a bowl and pour over boiling water until just covered. Leave until all the water has been absorbed, for about 8–10 minutes, then mix in the butter and fluff up with a fork.

❷ Meanwhile, heat half the oil in a heavy-based frying pan and add the onion and sauté for about 7 minutes, until softened. Add the chicken, garlic, cumin and coriander and cook, stirring occasionally, for a further 5–8 minutes, until the chicken is cooked and tender.

❸ Carefully mix in the couscous, peach and almonds and heat through gently, stirring the mixture occasionally.

Mini Meatballs in Tomato Sauce

PREPARATION TIME *10 minutes* **COOKING TIME** *30 minutes*

FREEZING *suitable* **MAKES** *2 portions*

These succulent meatballs are very versatile and make excellent burgers. Here, they are cooked in a rich tomato sauce.

INGREDIENTS
MEATBALLS
12 g/½ oz fresh breadcrumbs
25 g/1 oz cup freshly grated Parmesan cheese, plus extra for the topping
140 g/5 oz good-quality mince
1 small egg, beaten
1 small clove garlic, crushed (optional)
TOMATO SAUCE
1 tsp olive oil
1 small onion, finely chopped
300 ml/½ pint chopped tomatoes
1 bay leaf
1 tsp tomato purée
½ tsp dried oregano

❶ To make the meatballs, place all the ingredients in a blender and process until combined and formed into a smooth mixture. Shape the mixture into small balls. Set aside in the fridge.

❷ To make the tomato sauce, heat the oil in a small heavy-based frying pan. Add the onion and sauté for 7 minutes, until softened and translucent. Add the chopped tomatoes, bay leaf, tomato purée and oregano.

❸ Add the meatballs and simmer, half covered, for 20 minutes, or until the meatballs are cooked. Turn the meatballs occasionally during cooking. Remove the bay leaf and sprinkle the balls with more Parmesan, if liked.

Muffin Pizzas

PREPARATION TIME *10 minutes* **COOKING TIME** *20 minutes*
FREEZING *suitable* **MAKES** *2 portions*

I've used muffins as a base for these simple pizzas but you could try focaccia, a wholemeal bap or pitta bread. Toppings can be equally varied: choose from tomato, mozzarella cheese, sweetcorn, pepper, salami, chopped olives, strips of ham or tuna.

INGREDIENTS
1 tsp olive oil
½ clove garlic, crushed
90 ml/3 fl oz chopped tomatoes
1 tsp dried oregano
1–2 wholemeal/white muffins, halved
20 g/¾ o/z Cheddar cheese, grated
40 g/1½ oz mozzarella cheese, sliced

1. Preheat the oven to 200°C/400°F/Gas Mark 6. Heat the olive oil in a saucepan. Add the garlic and fry for 1 minute, until softened but not browned. Add the tomatoes and oregano. Cook over a low heat, stirring occasionally, for 5–8 minutes, or until reduced and thickened.

2. Spoon a little tomato sauce over each muffin half, then sprinkle the Cheddar and mozzarella cheeses over the top.

3. Place the muffins on a baking sheet and bake in the oven for 10 minutes, or until the topping is bubbling and golden.

Green Fingers

PREPARATION TIME *10 minutes*

FREEZING *suitable* **MAKES** *2 portions*

Serve this creamy, garlicky guacamole dip with soft, floury tortillas and sticks of steamed or raw carrot, pepper, cucumber, baby sweetcorn and mangetout. A spoonful of guacamole also makes a nutritious addition to soups and stews.

❶ Put the avocado, garlic and lemon juice into a bowl. Mash with a fork until fairly smooth and creamy.

❷ Warm the tortillas in a large dry frying pan. Spread the guacamole over the tortillas and cut into fingers or wedges, or roll them up.

INGREDIENTS
2 soft tortillas
GUACAMOLE
½ avocado, stoned and flesh scooped out
½ clove garlic, crushed
squeeze of fresh lemon juice

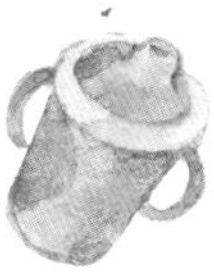

Pink Pasta Salad

PREPARATION TIME *10 minutes* **COOKING TIME** *10–15 minutes*
FREEZING *unsuitable* **MAKES** *2–4 portions*

Salad may not spring to mind as a suitable infant food but this one may change your ideas, and a novel-shaped pasta will add to its appeal. The choice of salad ingredients can also be varied according to your baby's likes and dislikes.

INGREDIENTS
85 g/3 oz fun-shaped pasta
½ small red pepper, seeded and diced
2 tomatoes, seeded and diced
2 tbsp canned sweetcorn, drained and rinsed
1–2 slices of ham or 1 cooked sausage, diced (optional)
2 tbsp red pesto
1–2 tbsp mayonnaise

1. Cook the pasta according to the instructions on the packet, until the pasta is tender. Drain and set aside.

2. Steam the pepper for 2 minutes, until softened.

3. Place the pasta, pepper, tomatoes, sweetcorn and ham, if using, in a bowl. Mix together the pesto and mayonnaise and spoon the mixture over the salad ingredients. Mix everything together well to coat all the ingredients in the sauce.

Coconut Muesli

PREPARATION TIME *10 minutes*

FREEZING *unsuitable* **MAKES** *10 portions*

This healthy breakfast of oats, nuts and dried fruit can double up as a nutritious pudding. For babies up to 12 months, serve the oaty cereal with breast or formula milk, allowing it to soften first in the milk before serving. Alternatively, soak the muesli in a little apple juice or water to soften the oats and stir a spoonful into natural yogurt.

1. Mix together the oats, wheat flakes, raisins, apricots, hazelnuts and coconut. Store the mixture in an airtight container.

2. Just before serving, mix a few spoonfuls of the muesli with 2 tablespoons of freshly grated apple, if liked.

INGREDIENTS
115 g/4 oz porridge oats
115 g/4 oz wheat flakes
3 tbsp raisins
55 g/2 oz dried unsulphured apricots, finely chopped
55 g/2 oz roasted hazelnuts, finely chopped
25 g/1 oz desiccated coconut
freshly grated apple (optional)

Sunny Honey Sundae

PREPARATION TIME *10 minutes* **COOKING TIME** *3 minutes*
FREEZING *unsuitable* **MAKES** *2–4 portions*

Named after the vibrant colour of the mango and orange purée, this pretty pudding is also good served with thick natural yogurt instead of the ice cream.

INGREDIENTS
1 orange, peeled and segmented
1 small mango, peeled, stoned and chopped
1–2 tbsp honey, according to taste
1 tbsp water
2–4 scoops vanilla ice cream
1–2 digestive biscuits, crushed

1. Put three-quarters of the orange and mango in a small heavy-based saucepan and add the honey and water. Bring to the boil, then reduce the heat and simmer for 2 minutes, or until the fruit has softened. You may need to add a little extra water if the fruit seems too dry.

2. Transfer the fruit to a blender and purée until smooth. Press the fruit through a sieve to remove any fibres or membranes, if necessary.

3. Place the reserved fruit in a serving bowl and top with a scoop of ice cream. Spoon over the orange and mango purée and sprinkle with the crushed biscuits. Yogurt can be used in the place of ice cream.

Banana Cinnamon Toast

PREPARATION TIME *5 minutes* **COOKING TIME** *3 minutes*
FREEZING *unsuitable* **MAKES** *1 portion*

A melt-in-the-mouth pudding or breakfast, which is popular with children and adults alike. Wholemeal toast, pannetone or fruit bread are just as delicious as the muffins used here.

INGREDIENTS
1 tbsp unsalted butter
1 small banana, peeled and sliced diagonally
2 tbsp maple syrup
¼ tsp ground cinnamon
sprinkling of chopped toasted almonds, to serve (optional)
½ fruit muffin, toasted
1 tbsp Greek-style yogurt, to serve

1. Melt the butter in a small heavy-based frying pan. Add the banana pieces and cook for 1 minute, turning to coat them in the butter.

2. Add the maple syrup and cinnamon and cook the banana for 1–2 minutes, until softened. Gently stir in the toasted almonds, if using.

3. Cut the toasted fruit muffin into fingers or wedges and spoon over the cooked banana. Serve with the Greek-style yogurt, either as a topping or on the side.

Baked Apple Crumblies

PREPARATION TIME *10 minutes* **COOKING TIME** *45 minutes*
FREEZING *unsuitable* **MAKES** *4–8 portions*

This variation on the classic apple crumble uses whole apples, which are filled with dried fruit and topped with an oaty crumble. Serve the apples with custard, cream or ice cream.

INGREDIENTS
4 small cooking apples, such as Bramley
40 g/1½ oz plain flour, sifted
2 tbsp unsalted butter, cubed
2 tbsp porridge oats
3 tbsp soft light brown sugar
55 g/2 oz dried, ready-to-eat dates, stoned and finely chopped
25 g/1 oz raisins

❶ Preheat the oven to 180°C/350°F/Gas Mark 4. Core each apple and score the skin around the circumference to prevent the apples bursting during baking.

❷ Put the flour and butter in a bowl and, using your fingertips, rub into coarse breadcrumbs. Add the oats and sugar and mix well. Combine the dates and raisins in a separate bowl.

❸ Half fill the cavity of each apple with the dried fruit, then top with the crumble mixture.

❹ Place the apples in an ovenproof dish and pour in a little water. Bake for 45 minutes, until the apples are tender.

Chocolate Cinnamon Rice Pudding

PREPARATION TIME *5 minutes* **COOKING TIME** *2 hours*

FREEZING *suitable* **MAKES** *4 portions*

Yummy! The ultimate comfort food, this rice pudding is even more delicious topped with sliced bananas or finely chopped roasted almonds or hazelnuts.

INGREDIENTS
600 ml/1 pint full cream milk
3 tsp good quality cocoa powder
70 g/2½ oz pudding rice
3 tsp caster sugar
½ tsp ground cinnamon

❶ Preheat the oven to 160°C/325°F/Gas Mark 3. Warm the milk and cocoa powder in a saucepan over a low heat. Whisk until the cocoa blends into the milk, then remove from the heat.

❷ Place the rice in a small ovenproof dish, then pour in the chocolate milk. Sprinkle with the sugar and cinnamon and stir everything together well.

❸ Cover the dish and bake in the oven for 2 hours, or until most of the milk has been absorbed and the rice is very tender. Leave to cool slightly before serving.

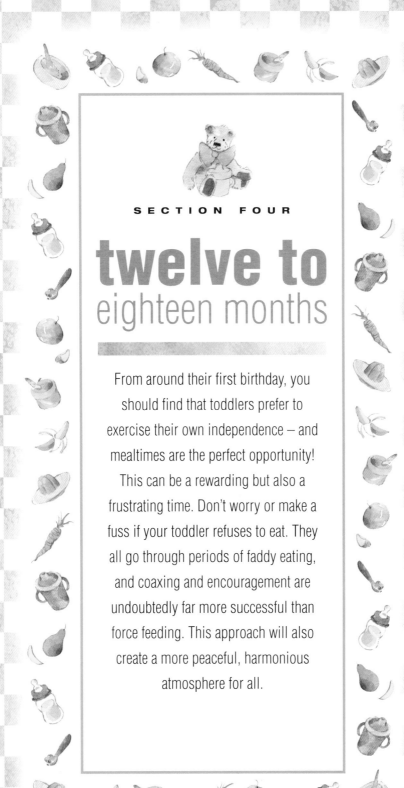

SECTION FOUR

twelve to eighteen months

From around their first birthday, you should find that toddlers prefer to exercise their own independence – and mealtimes are the perfect opportunity! This can be a rewarding but also a frustrating time. Don't worry or make a fuss if your toddler refuses to eat. They all go through periods of faddy eating, and coaxing and encouragement are undoubtedly far more successful than force feeding. This approach will also create a more peaceful, harmonious atmosphere for all.

A Fussy Eater

Toddlers inevitably turn their noses up at some foods presented to them, but the best way to deal with fads and picky eating is to ignore them, however difficult and frustrating this may be. Habits are formed early, so stick to your guns and try to encourage your toddler to experience a variety of foods – encompassing a range of flavours, colours and textures – so they get used to trying new things.

HEALTHY CHOICE

Many of us have the preconceived idea that toddlers prefer bland, mushy foods, and consequently resort to so-called 'children's food'. Researchers at the University of Birmingham, however, have discovered that toddlers are far more open to new tastes and stronger flavours than previously thought. The popularity of garlic bread, houmus and garlic butter is testimony to this.

While it is not always feasible for the family to eat together, you will reap the benefits even if you only manage communal mealtimes at weekends. Although the target is to encourage your toddler to eat the same foods as the rest of the family, a high-fibre, low-fat diet is unsuitable for young children. Instead provide a good balance of high-energy, nutrient-dense foods, including plenty of fruit and vegetables, full-fat dairy produce, carbohydrates in the form of breads, pasta, potatoes and rice, as well as protein foods, including lean meat, poultry, fish, beans, eggs and different vegetarian alternatives.

FUSSY EATING

If your toddler happily eats everything that is presented to him or her, then you really are extremely lucky and are likely to be in the minority. Toddlers of this age are too busy or distracted to sit down and eat. A simple way around this is to give your child his or her own spoon and bowl containing a little food, while you give the majority of the meal to the family. (Smaller portions are less off-putting.) Finger foods are also popular and will allow your toddler his or her desired independence or enable him or her to play with a toy while eating.

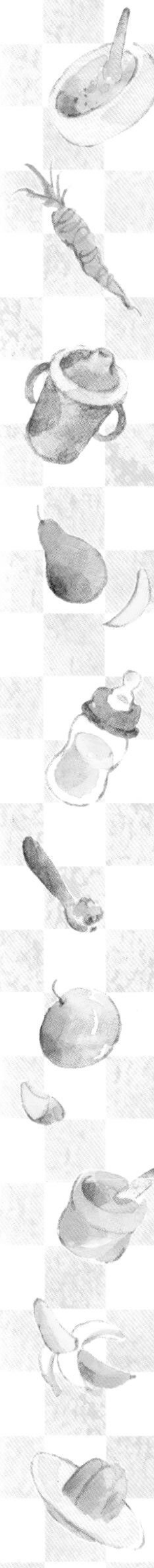

Toddlers can be incredibly fickle, loving a certain food one day and disliking it the next, and their appetite can be equally unpredictable. Again, try not to let this concern you.

Imaginative presentation can also make the difference. This doesn't mean spending hours creating complicated pictures out of every meal, but do try to choose different coloured and textured foods and arrange them in an attractive pattern. Brightly coloured plates can also help to make eating fun.

MILK AND DRINKS

Cow's milk can be given as a drink at this stage, as well as used in cooking. While you may still be breastfeeding, it is no longer necessary to provide formula or follow-on milk, but this does mean that you should take care to ensure that your toddler's diet contains the required vitamins, minerals, fat, protein and carbohydrates.

ABOVE *Making mealtimes fun and less threatening can result in a less fussy child who is willing to try new foods.*

RECIPES

The recipes in this chapter have been created to appeal to toddlers and adults alike with the odd concession to healthy versions of so-called 'children's food'. I've tried to include a wide collection of dishes incorporating a range of flavours and textures. If time allows, encourage your toddler to get involved in the preparation of meals – it can be a fun time for the whole family.

MEAL PLANNER 4

12-18 MONTHS	BREAKFAST	LUNCH
		(with diluted unsweetened fruit juice – 1 part juice: 5 parts water – or cooled boiled water)
Day 1	Granola, toast, milk	Vegetable & chickpea coconut cur Quick summer pudding
Day 2	Boiled egg Soldiers with yeast extract, yogurt, milk	Cottage pie & French beans Apple sponge pudding
Day 3	Coconut muesli Muffin, milk	Oodles of noodles Fromage frais & mango
Day 4	Weetabix & banana Toast, milk	Gammon & pineapple rice, broccoli Baked apple crumblies
Day 5	Poached egg & beans Soda bread, milk	Two-fish pasta bake, vegetables Chocolate cinnamon rice pudding
Day 6	Porridge, toast, milk	Moroccan chicken couscous Vegetables Sunset jelly
Day 7	Scotch pancakes & fruit Yogurt, milk	Mini meatballs in tomato sauce Rice & vegetables Sunny honey sundae

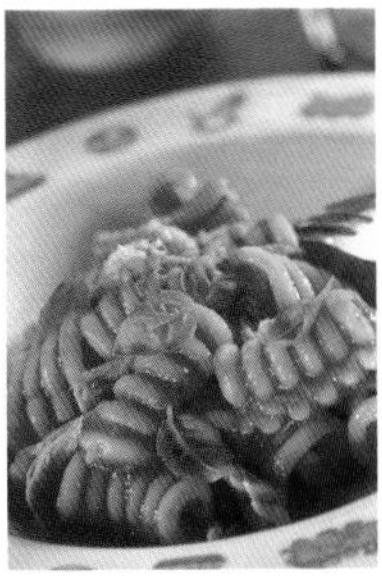

TEA	SUPPER	BEDTIME
(same drink as lunch)	(same drink as tea)	
Quick tuna pasta & broccoli Sunny honey sundae	Banana cinnamon toast Fruit	Milk
Minestrone soup Garlic bread Strawberry yogurt lolly	Muffin pizza Fruit	Milk
Baked plaice with tomato rice, vegetables Apple & coconut cookies	Scrambled egg on toast Fruit	Milk
Creamy tomato soup Wholemeal bread Yogurt	Green fingers Pitta bread Grated cheese, fruit	Milk
Pink pasta salad Breadsticks Apple & coconut cookies	Sandwich Fruit	Milk
Creamy salmon & broccoli pasta Strawberry yogurt lolly	Cheese on toast Fruit	Milk
Pesto potatoes Grated carrot Banana yogurt custard	Houmus, vegetable sticks, tortilla Fruit	Milk

Vegetable & Chickpea Coconut Curry

PREPARATION TIME *10 minutes* **COOKING TIME** *30 minutes*

FREEZING *suitable* **MAKES** *4–6 portions*

I've found this mild and creamy curry goes down particularly well with older babies. For adults, bump up the quantity of spices.

INGREDIENTS

- 3 new potatoes, peeled and quartered
- 8 small cauliflower florets
- 2 tsp vegetable oil
- 1 small clove garlic, chopped
- 1 tsp garam masala
- ½ tsp turmeric
- 200 ml/7 fl oz hot vegetable stock
- 35 g/1¼ oz creamed coconut, chopped into small pieces
- 2 tomatoes, seeded and chopped
- 1 tbsp tomato purée
- small handful of spinach leaves, tough stalks removed and finely shredded
- 4 tbsp canned chickpeas, drained and rinsed

1. Cook the potatoes in boiling water for 10 minutes, or until tender. Add the cauliflower to the potatoes 5 minutes before the end of the cooking time.

2. Meanwhile, heat the oil in a heavy-based saucepan, add the garlic and sauté for 1 minute, until softened but not coloured. Mix in the spices and cook.

3. Put the vegetable stock and creamed coconut into a jug and stir until the coconut has dissolved. Add the stock mixture to the pan with the fresh tomatoes and tomato purée. Cook for 15 minutes, stirring occasionally, until thickened.

4. Add the spinach and chickpeas to the pan and cook for 2 minutes, until the spinach is tender. Add the potatoes and cauliflower and heat through. Mash or chop.

Two-Fish Pasta Bake

PREPARATION TIME *10 minutes* **COOKING TIME** *45 minutes*

FREEZING *suitable* **MAKES** *4–6 portions*

This fish pie is topped with pasta and mozzarella cheese rather than mashed potato.

INGREDIENTS

85 g/3 oz penne or macaroni
2 tsp olive oil, plus extra for coating pasta
1 egg
1 small onion, finely chopped
1 small celery stick, finely chopped
1 small carrot, peeled and finely chopped
small handful of spinach leaves, tough stalks removed and finely shredded
120 ml/4 fl oz full cream milk
2 tbsp double cream
25 g/1 oz mature Cheddar cheese, grated
½ tsp English mustard
1 tbsp finely chopped fresh parsley
squeeze of fresh lemon juice
90 g/3¼ oz undyed smoked haddock, skin and bones removed
140 g/5 oz cod fillet, skin and bones removed
85 g/3 oz mozzarella cheese, broken into small pieces

❶ Preheat the oven to 200°C/400°F/Gas Mark 6. Cook the pasta according to the instructions on the packet until tender. Drain well. Toss in oil.

❷ Bring a small saucepan of water to the boil and add the egg. Cook for 8–10 minutes, until the egg is hard boiled. Cool the egg under cold running water.

❸ Heat the oil in a heavy-based frying pan. Add the onion and sauté for 5 minutes, until softened, then add the celery and carrot and sauté for 3 minutes. Add the spinach and cook for a further 2 minutes, until tender.

❹ Stir in the milk and cream and bring to the boil. Turn off the heat and stir in the Cheddar cheese, mustard, parsley and lemon juice.

❺ Place the fish in a small ovenproof dish. Shell and chop the egg and spoon it over the fish, then top with the sauce. Arrange the pasta over the top and sprinkle with the mozzarella cheese. Bake for 20–25 minutes, or until the fish is cooked and the top has browned.

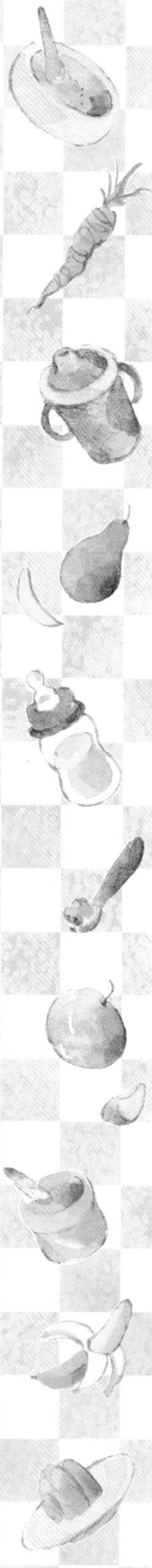

Oodles of Noodles

PREPARATION TIME *10 minutes* **COOKING TIME** *15 minutes*
FREEZING *unsuitable* **MAKES** *4–6 portions*

Noodles are both fun and versatile, so it's no surprise that they're loved by children. Although peanuts, used here in the satay sauce, are nutritious and sustaining, take care when introducing them to your baby's diet as increasing numbers of people are finding that they are allergic to nuts.

INGREDIENTS
8 broccoli florets, cut into small florets
85 g/3 oz medium egg noodles
2 tsp vegetable oil
1 small clove garlic, chopped
1 tsp grated fresh root ginger
¼ tsp ground coriander
1 skinless chicken breast, cut into strips
4 fine French beans, finely sliced
15 g/½ oz creamed coconut, cut into small pieces
50 ml/2 fl oz hot water
2 heaped tbsp smooth peanut butter
squeeze of fresh lemon juice
55 g/2 oz canned sweetcorn, drained and rinsed
2 tsp soy sauce

1. Steam the broccoli for 8 minutes, or until just tender. Meanwhile, cook the noodles according to the instructions on the packet, until tender, then drain and cool under cold running water.

2. At the same time, heat the oil in a wok or heavy-based frying pan. Add the garlic, ginger and coriander and sauté for 1 minute, stirring continuously. Add the chicken and French beans and stir-fry for a further 5–8 minutes, until the chicken is cooked.

3. Mix together the coconut, water and peanut butter until combined, then pour the mixture over the chicken. Cook for 3 minutes, or until reduced and thickened.

4. Add the noodles, broccoli, lemon juice, sweetcorn and soy sauce and heat through, stirring continuously. Chop to the desired consistency, if necessary.

VARIATION

Replace the chicken with a handful of cooked prawns, adding them with the noodles in step 4. The beans can be replaced with peas.

Gammon & Pineapple Rice

PREPARATION TIME *10 minutes* **COOKING TIME** *20 minutes*

FREEZING *unsuitable* **MAKES** *2 portions*

A classic combination of ham and pineapple is presented in this baby-friendly dish. Sweetcorn is added for sweetness and bite.

INGREDIENTS
55 g/2 oz long-grain rice, rinsed
250 ml/8 fl oz water
1 thick gammon steak
runny honey, for glazing
2 tbsp unsalted butter
3 tbsp sweetcorn, drained and rinsed
85 g/3 oz fresh pineapple, cubed
1 tbsp finely chopped fresh parsley

❶ Place the rice in a saucepan. Cover with the water and bring to the boil. Reduce the heat, cover, and simmer for 15 minutes, until the water has been absorbed and the rice is cooked.

❷ Meanwhile, heat the grill to high. Brush the gammon with honey and grill for 8–10 minutes on each side, until cooked through. Cut the meat into bite-sized pieces.

❸ At the same time, melt the butter in a small heavy-based saucepan and add the sweetcorn and pineapple and heat through for a minute or so. Add the rice, gammon and parsley to the pan and stir well to combine.

Cottage Pie

PREPARATION TIME *10 minutes* **COOKING TIME** *45 minutes*
FREEZING *suitable* **MAKES** *4–6 portions*

This is always a favourite and can be made with meat or vegetarian alternatives, such as soya or Quorn mince.

INGREDIENTS
2 tsp olive oil
1 small onion, finely chopped
1 small clove garlic, finely chopped
1 courgette, diced
1 carrot, peeled and diced
3 mushrooms, peeled and finely chopped
½ tsp oregano
½ tsp thyme
1 bay leaf
115 g/4 oz lean mince, soya or Quorn mince
3 tbsp canned cannellini beans, drained and rinsed
150 ml/¼ pint vegetable stock
150 ml/¼ pint chopped tomatoes
1 tbsp tomato purée
2 potatoes, peeled and cubed
1 heaped tbsp unsalted butter
2–3 tbsp full cream milk
25 g/1 oz Cheddar cheese, grated

❶ Preheat the oven to 180°C/350°F/Gas Mark 4. Heat the oil in a heavy-based saucepan. Add the onion and garlic and sauté for 5 minutes until softened. Add the courgette, carrot, mushrooms and herbs and cook for a further 5 minutes, until the vegetables have softened. Add the mince and cook until browned, stirring occasionally.

❷ Add the cannellini beans, stock, chopped tomatoes and tomato purée to the mince and bring to the boil, then reduce the heat and simmer, half covered, for 10–15 minutes, until the sauce has thickened and reduced.

❸ Meanwhile, cook the potatoes in boiling water for 15 minutes, or until tender. Drain well. Add the butter and milk to the potato and mash until smooth.

❹ Put the mince mixture into an ovenproof casserole dish and spoon the mash over the top. Sprinkle the grated cheese over the top and bake in the oven for 20 minutes, until the cheese has melted and the top is golden.

Creamy Tomato Soup with Garlic Croutons

PREPARATION TIME *10 minutes* **COOKING TIME** *45 minutes*
FREEZING *suitable* **MAKES** *6 portions*

Remarkably, children who turn their noses up at vegetables will happily eat them in this liquidised form.

INGREDIENTS
GARLIC CROUTONS
2 tbsp olive oil
2 cloves garlic, peeled and halved
3 slices white bread or French stick, crusts removed
1 tbsp olive oil
1 onion, chopped
1 carrot, peeled and finely chopped
1 small potato, peeled and cubed
500-g/1¼-lb carton creamed tomatoes
400 ml/14 fl oz vegetable stock

❶ Preheat the oven to 200°C/400°F/Gas Mark 6. To make the garlic croutons, rub both sides of each slice of bread with the garlic. Cut the bread into cubes and put them into a small plastic bag with the olive oil. Shake the bag to coat the bread in the oil. Place the bread cubes on a baking sheet and bake for 10–12 minutes, until crisp and golden – keep an eye on the croutons as they burn easily.

❷ To make the soup, heat the oil in a heavy-based saucepan. Add the onion, cover the pan, and sweat for 10 minutes, until softened. Add the carrot and potato and sweat for a further 2 minutes, stirring occasionally to prevent the vegetables sticking.

❸ Add the creamed tomatoes and stock and bring to the boil. Reduce the heat and simmer, half covered, for 25 minutes, until the vegetables are tender and the liquid has reduced and thickened.

❹ Carefully pour the mixture into a blender (or use a hand-held one) and process until smooth and creamy. Return the soup to the pan and heat through if necessary. Sprinkle with the croutons before serving.

Quick Tuna Pasta

PREPARATION TIME *5 minutes* **COOKING TIME** *15 minutes*

FREEZING *suitable* **MAKES** *2 portions*

Tinned tuna and dried pasta are great storecupboard standbys and lend themselves to a multitude of dishes. The sugar helps to reduce the acidity of the tomatoes but it can be omitted if preferred.

INGREDIENTS
85 g/3 oz pasta shapes
2 tsp olive oil
1 small clove garlic, finely chopped
3 tbsp white wine (optional)
175 ml/6 fl oz passata
pinch of sugar (optional)
sprig of fresh basil
small tin tuna fish in oil, drained
1 tbsp fromage frais or houmus

1. Cook the pasta according to the instructions on the packet until tender, then drain well.

2. Meanwhile, heat the oil in a heavy-based saucepan. Add the garlic and sauté for 1 minute, until softened, stirring to prevent it sticking to the pan and burning. Pour in the wine, if using, and boil for a minute to allow the alcohol to evaporate.

3. Reduce the heat to medium, add the passata, sugar, basil and tuna to the pan and cook for a further 8–10 minutes, until the sauce has thickened and reduced. Stir in the fromage frais and warm over a low heat for a minute or so. Remove the sprig of basil and spoon the sauce over the pasta or mix the two together well. You can sprinkle cheese on top, if liked.

Pesto Potatoes

PREPARATION TIME *15 minutes* **COOKING TIME** *1–1½ hours*

FREEZING *unsuitable* **MAKES** *1 portions*

Baked potatoes have a lot going for them as they are easy to prepare, are filling and provide fibre, vitamins and minerals. I've included a recipe for pesto here but you could use a ready-made one if preferred. If you do make your own, you can store it in an airtight jar in the refrigerator for up to a week.

INGREDIENTS

- 1 small baking potato, scrubbed
- handful of spinach leaves, shredded
- 1 tbsp freshly grated Cheddar or Parmesan cheese

PESTO

- 25 g/1 oz fresh basil leaves
- 1 clove garlic, crushed
- 15 g/¾ oz pine kernels
- 4 tbsp olive oil
- 2 tbsp freshly grated Parmesan cheese

1. Preheat the oven to 200°C/400°F/Gas Mark 6. Bake the potato for 1–1½ hours, until it is tender.

2. To make the pesto, place the basil, garlic and pine kernels in a blender and process until finely chopped. Gradually add the olive oil and then the Parmesan cheese and blend to a coarse purée.

3. Steam the spinach for 3 minutes, or until tender. Squeeze out any excess water and chop.

4. Cut the potato in half and scoop out most of the flesh, reserving the skins. Put the potato flesh in a bowl with 2 tablespoons of pesto and the spinach and mash until combined. Spoon the pesto mixture back into the potato skins and sprinkle with the Cheddar cheese.

5. Place the potatoes under a hot grill for a minute or two until the cheese is bubbling and golden.

Granola

PREPARATION TIME *5 minutes* **COOKING TIME** *55 minutes*
FREEZING *unsuitable* **MAKES** *10 portions*

This honey-coated crunchy cereal contains none of the additives or large amounts of sugar found in many commercial alternatives. For young babies, soak the cereal in milk or fruit juice before serving or alternatively grind in a blender to the desired texture. A spoonful can also be mixed into natural yogurt.

INGREDIENTS

115 g/4 oz porridge oats
25 g/1 oz sunflower seeds
25 g/1 oz sesame seeds
50 g/2 oz roasted hazelnuts, finely chopped
3 tbsp sunflower oil
3 tbsp runny honey
50 g/2 oz raisins
50 g/2 oz dried, ready-to-eat apples, finely chopped

❶ Preheat the oven to 140°C/275°F/Gas Mark 1. Mix the oats, seeds and nuts together in a bowl.

❷ Heat the oil and honey in a saucepan until melted, then remove from the heat, add the oat mixture and stir well. Place the honey-coated oat mixture on two baking sheets in one layer.

❸ Cook for 50 minutes, or until crisp, stirring occasionally to prevent the mixture sticking to the baking sheets. Remove from the oven and mix in the raisins and dried apple. Allow to cool and store in an airtight container.

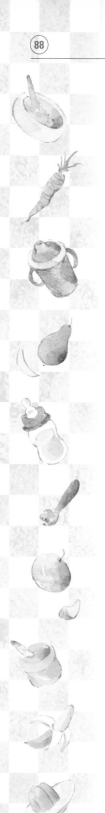

Apple Sponge Pudding

PREPARATION TIME *15 minutes* **COOKING TIME** *40 minutes*

FREEZING *unsuitable* **MAKES** *6 portions*

This combination of tender cooked apples and vanilla sponge topping is delicious served cold with a scoop of ice cream.

INGREDIENTS

650 g/1 lb 7oz cooking apples, peeled, cored and sliced

100 g/3½ oz caster sugar

2 tbsp water

½ tsp ground cinnamon

6 tbsp margarine, softened

2 eggs, beaten

½ tsp vanilla essence

85 g/3 oz self-raising flour, sifted

❶ Preheat the oven to 180°C/350°F/Gas Mark 4. Place the apples, 2 tablespoons of the sugar and the water in a heavy-based saucepan. Cover and cook over a low heat for 4–5 minutes, until the apples have softened. Stir in the cinnamon and transfer to an ovenproof dish.

❷ To make the sponge, beat the margarine with the remaining sugar using a wooden spoon, or process in a blender until light and creamy. Add the eggs, vanilla essence and flour. Beat or process to a soft, creamy consistency.

❸ Spoon the sponge mixture over the apples and smooth it down gently with the back of a spoon. Bake for 30–35 minutes, until the sponge is risen and golden and springy to the touch.

Quick Summer Pudding

PREPARATION TIME *15 minutes* **COOKING TIME** *5 minutes*

FREEZING *suitable* **MAKES** *2–4 portions*

The classic summer pudding should be left overnight but this version tastes just as good and takes a fraction of the time to prepare. I've used pastry cutters to form the bread into fun shapes, but make sure they are the same size as the bread slices as small shapes will end up as a soggy, fruit-soaked mass.

❶ Put the berries in a saucepan with the sugar and water. Bring to the boil, then reduce the heat and simmer for 5 minutes, or until the fruit is soft and juicy.

❷ Cut the bread into your chosen shape(s) – make sure you have 2 of each shape – using a large pastry cutter. (The cutter should use as much of the bread slice as possible to avoid wastage.)

❸ Place half the bread shapes in a shallow dish, then spoon over the warm fruit. Place the remaining bread shapes on top of the fruit and bread, then spoon over the warm juice until covered. Press down lightly to soak the syrup into the bread. Leave for about 30 minutes before serving.

INGREDIENTS
450 g/1 lb mixed berries, such as strawberries, raspberries, blackcurrants or blackberries, hulled and the large fruit sliced
4–6 slices day-old white bread, crusts removed
4–5 tbsp caster sugar, according to taste
5 tbsp water
pastry cutters, such as hearts, stars or gingerbread people

Strawberry Yogurt Lollies

PREPARATION TIME *5 minutes* **FREEZING** *suitable* **MAKES** 6

I've chosen strawberries because they are universally popular with children, but other types of fruit also go down well. The lollies are basically a frozen fruit smoothie, so they can be served in their unfrozen form too.

1. Put the strawberries, yogurt, honey and vanilla essence in a blender and process until puréed.

INGREDIENTS

350 g/12 oz fresh strawberries, hulled and sliced

300 g/10½ oz thick natural yogurt

3 tbsp honey

few drops of vanilla essence

VARIATION

Most types of soft fruit can be used to make frozen lollies. Try raspberries, mango, peaches, nectarines, plums or melon, or try a combination of fruits.

2. Pour the mixture into ice lolly moulds and freeze until solid. (Fun-shaped moulds are popular.)

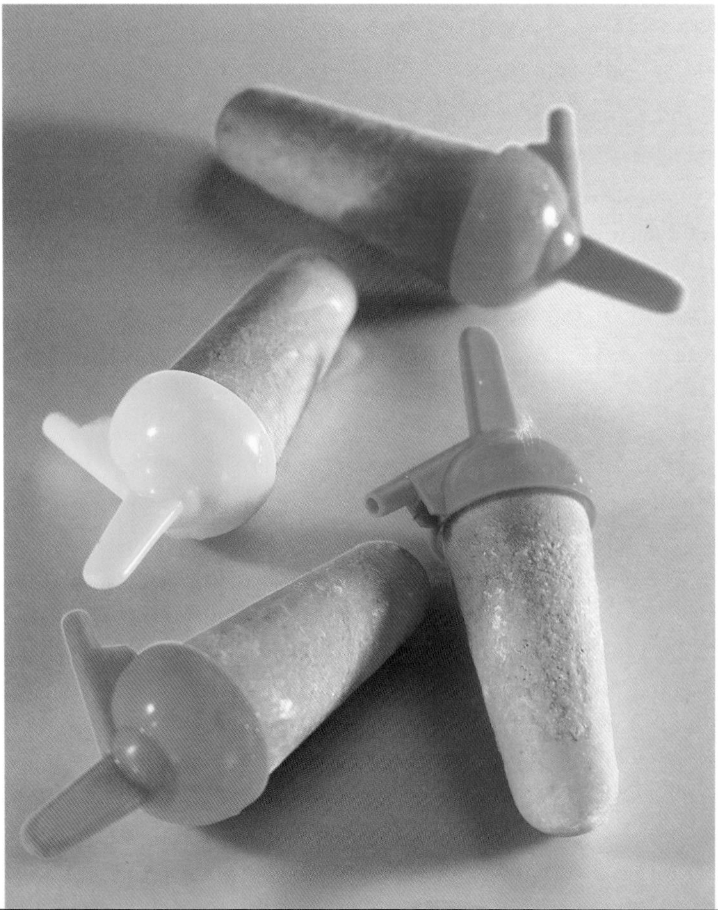

Apple & Coconut Cookies

PREPARATION TIME *15 minutes* **COOKING TIME** *20 minutes*

FREEZING *unsuitable* **MAKES** *12*

These wholesome cookies have a soft, chewy texture, rather like flapjacks. Store in an airtight jar.

INGREDIENTS
115 g/4 oz unsalted butter, plus extra for greasing
85 g/3 oz caster sugar
2 tbsp golden syrup
2 eating apples, cored and grated
115 g/4 oz wholemeal self-raising flour
3 tbsp desiccated coconut
115 g/4 oz porridge oats

❶ Preheat the oven to 180°C/350°F/Gas Mark 4. Lightly grease 2 large baking sheets. Put the butter, sugar and syrup in a small saucepan. Cook over a gentle heat, until the butter melts and the sugar dissolves, stirring occasionally. Remove the pan from the heat.

❷ Put the grated apple, flour, coconut and oats in a large bowl, then add the syrup mixture. Mix with a wooden spoon to form a sticky dough. Place large spoonfuls of the mixture on the prepared baking sheets to make 12 cookies. Form the mixture into rounds, about 5 cm/2 in in diameter, leaving plenty of space around each one to allow them to spread whilst cooking.

❸ Bake for 15 minutes, or until golden and slightly crisp. Leave to cool slightly on the baking sheets, then transfer the cookies to a wire rack to cool.

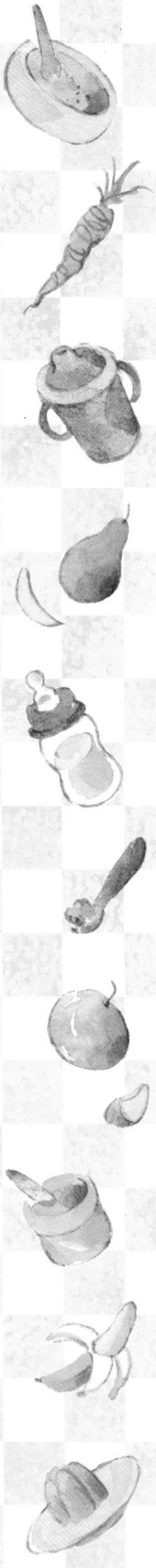

Useful Websites and Organisations

The following information is useful if you want some more information of weaning, or any medical aspect of childcare.

USEFUL WEBSITES

www.planetmedica.co.uk
This site is useful for additional information on weaning and how to go about it.

www.kidshealth.org
Large sections on "Feeding your newborn," "Feeding your 1–3 month old," "Feeding your 4–7 month old," and "Feeding your 8–12 month old." Plus useful question and answer sections, detailing topics you might have queries about, and the usual chat rooms for informal research.

www.allhealth.com
Good information on weaning; starting solids; baby food; finger food; fluids and juices; feeding methods; nutritional guidelines; and how to deal with picky eaters.

www.babyworld.co.uk
Good information on what first foods to offer between 4 to 6 months; feeding from 6 to 9 months; feeding from 12 months on; food intolerances and common food allergies; vegetarian babies; vegan babies; special diets; vitamin supplements; organic baby foods tried and tested; and some baby recipes to try.

www.abcparenting.com
General information on coping with your newborn and the right time to introduce solids.

babyparenting.about.com
A selection of recipes for first foods and information on breastfeeding your newborn.

www.babycenter.com
Information on health and development, breastfeeding, introducing first foods, and nutritional guides.

www.parenttime.com
Chat forums you can visit to discuss any questions you may have with other mothers, and a chance to gather information and raise any queries and questions of your own about newborns.

firstyears.excite.com
Information on typical child development from newborns to 2-year-olds.

www.babyzone.com
General information on pregnancy and your newborn, covering breastfeeding and weaning.

www.family.go.com
A more general family site, which puts the arrival of a newborn in the context of the family group. How to deal with a new baby and breastfeeding, how to begin weaning and introduce new foods into your child's diet.

www.familyweb.com
Information on what to expect in the first minutes, days and weeks at home with your baby plus guidelines on feeding and general nutrition.

http://members.aol.com/parentspage/booklet.html
A guided tour of the newborn from head to toe, plus plenty of general information on growth, and feeding and bathing your baby.

www.parentsplace.com
Extensive resources relating to breastfeeding, including information for working mothers and weaning.

USEFUL ORGANISATIONS

Association of Breastfeeding Mothers
abm@clara.net
http://home.clara.net/abm/
Offers breastfeeding advice and information, and trains breastfeeding counsellors.

Beyond the Baby Blues
www.babyblues.freeserve.co.uk
Offers an easily accessible, confidential support network for mothers who are suffering from post-natal depression.

Centre for Pregnancy Nutrition
pregnancy.nutrition@sheffield.ac.uk
Helpline: (+44) 0114 2424084

Fathers Direct
www.fathersdirect.com
mail@fathersdirect.com
Promotes close and positive relationships between men and their children from infancy. Aims to break down barriers that exist in society that make it difficult for fathers to develop such relationships with their children.

Parentline Plus
www.parentline.co.uk
Helpline: (+44) 0808 800 2222
Offers support to anyone who is parenting a child – the child's parents, step-parents, grandparents and foster parents. Provides a range of information.

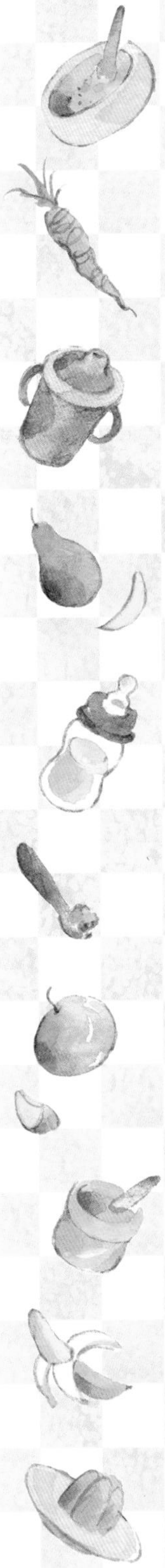

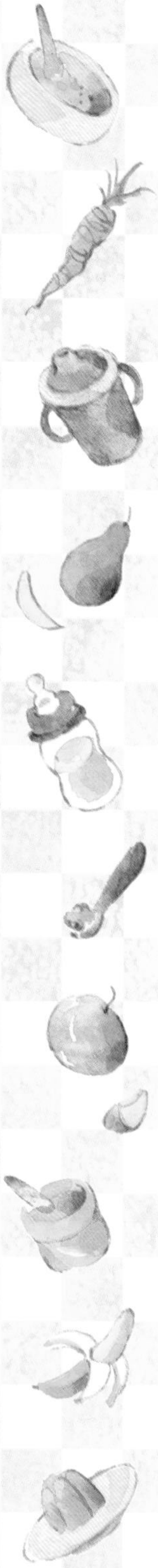

Index

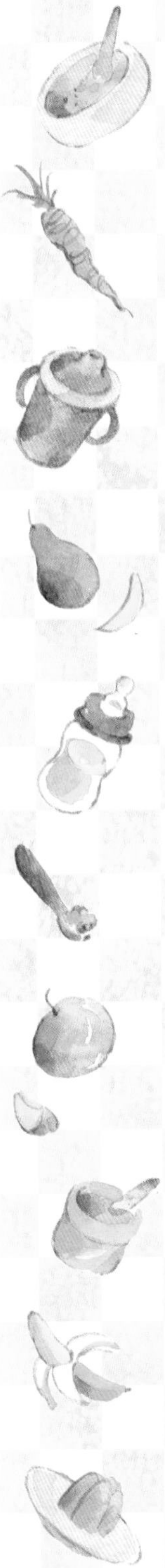

Acknowledgements

The author would like to thank the following:
The Institute of Child Health, London; The Health Education Authority, London; The Department of Health, London.

The publishers would like to thank the following for permission to reproduce copyright material: Bridgewater Book Company: p. 55; Getty Stone: p. 72; Image Bank: front cover, pp. 4, 5, 8, 9, 12, 32, 34, 52, 75; Superstock: p. 15.